faith-dipped
chocolate

faith-dipped chocolate

*Rich Encouragement
to Sweeten Your Day*

Louise Bergmann DuMont

Revell
Grand Rapids, Michigan

Published by Fleming H. Revell
a division of Baker Publishing Group
P.O. Box 6287, Grand Rapids, MI 49516-6287
www.revellbooks.com

Printed in the United States of America

Published in association with the literary agency of Janet Kobobel Grant, Books & Such, 4788 Carissa Ave., Santa Rosa, CA 95405.

Library of Congress Cataloging-in-Publication Data
DuMont, Louise Bergmann, 1953–
    Faith-dipped chocolate : rich encouragement to sweeten your day / Louise Bergmann DuMont.
        p.   cm.
    Includes bibliographical references.
    ISBN 0-8007-5944-3 (pbk.)
    1. Christian women—Religious life—Anecdotes. 2. Christian life—Anecdotes. I. Title.
    BV4527.D86 2005
    242'.643—dc22   2004014409

This book is dedicated to
my parents, Hermann and Irmgard Bergmann,
who instilled in me first,
a lifelong love for Christ my Savior . . .
and then, a true appreciation for good chocolate.

Hermann Bergmann
March 6, 1923–January 29, 2004

Las cosas claras y el chocolate espeso [Ideas should be clear and chocolate thick].

Spanish Proverb

Contents

Contents

1
Itchy Love

It was a warm summer afternoon filled with the smell of roasted hot dogs and the sound of kids playing kickball. The squeak of playground swings and the serenade of crickets rounded out our day in the park. My friend and I relaxed in our lawn chairs as we watched the men play one last game of ball with the kids before dusk routed their fun. My friend's daughter, too young for the competition on the field, busied herself with cartoon-filled coloring books and chunky, kid-friendly crayons.

"Mommy, I want a drink," the girl said, scratching vigorously at a mosquito bite on her arm as she left her amusements and came to where we sat.

Her mother popped the straw into a juice box from the cooler at our side. "Here you go," she said.

The girl took the box with one hand and scratched again with the other.

"Just a minute. I want to put something on that bite," my friend said, motioning her daughter to her side.

The youngster scrunched up her nose, drawing attention to a crop of cute freckles. "I hate mosquitoes," she said.

Her mom smiled in sympathy and gave the girl's nose a gentle tweak.

That's when it happened. The innocence of youth voiced a question that would only suggest itself to a child: "Mommy, does God love mosquitoes?"

I stifled a chuckle as I watched her mother's brow crease.

"Well, did God make mosquitoes?" she asked, stalling for time.

"Uh-huh," was her daughter's quick reply.

"Then God loves mosquitoes," her mother said, unable to come up with a more profound reply.

The child accepted her mother's answer without hesitation and returned to her play with nary another thought.

As the day drew to a close, our group gathered one last time to roast marshmallows and enjoy slices of homemade devil's food cake. My teenage sons passed up the time-consuming marshmallow roast and opted for huge chunks of cake slathered in dark chocolate frosting. Since my friend and I were watching our diets, we accepted only small slivers of the rich dessert.

"Wouldn't it be wonderful if chocolate had no calories?" my friend commented, allowing the pleasure of her last bite to register on her face.

I scraped some of the calorie-laden icing to the side of my plate, then lifted a forkful of moist cake to my lips. "The chocolate in this cake is what makes it so good! If chocolate had no calories, I think my boys would have to fight me to get near this cake."

My friend stared down at her plate and moaned, "I think I hate chocolate."

Like the whisper of a gentle breeze on a summer's eve, her daughter's small hand appeared over her shoulder and brushed her cheek. "Mommy, did God make chocolate?"

This time my chuckles weren't restrained, and a slight blush covered my friend's face. I trained my eyes on the chocolate cake but kept my ears eagerly tuned in to their conversation.

"Yes, honey, God did make chocolate."

I had three children of my own and knew full well the direction this conversation was about to take. I held my breath in anticipation.

"I guess that means God loves chocolate too, right, Mommy?"

"Yes, I guess he does," her mother replied, sighing deeply.

I looked up, and as our eyes met we allowed ourselves to smile.

> God saw everything that he had made, and indeed, it was very good.
>
> Genesis 1:31

Recipe to Relish

Brownie Pudding Cake

Main Ingredients

- 1 cup all-purpose flour
- ¾ cup sugar
- 4 Tbsp. unsweetened cocoa powder
- 2 tsp. baking powder
- ½ tsp. salt
- ½ cup milk
- 2 Tbsp. melted butter
- 1 tsp. vanilla

Topping

1 cup sugar
¼ cup unsweetened cocoa powder
1½ cups boiling water

Optional

whipped cream for garnishing

Preheat oven to 350 degrees. Combine the main ingredients and stir well with a wooden spoon. Do not use a mixer. Pour the mixture into a greased 9 x 9 baking dish. In a separate bowl, combine the sugar and cocoa for the topping. Gradually stir in the boiling water. Pour the topping over the mixture and bake for 45 minutes. Right before you serve this rich dessert, top each serving with a large dollop of whipped cream.

2

Caramel, Crème, or Jelly?

"Would you like a chocolate?" I asked my co-worker as I held out a box of assorted confections.

"Sure. What kind do you have?" she replied, peering over the edge.

What kind? I thought. *Does it matter?*

"It's an assortment," I replied. "I know there are truffles, nuts, crèmes—"

"I don't like chocolates with jelly filling," she interrupted.

"Oh!"

Ignoring my response, she asked, "Isn't there some rule about the square ones being caramels?"

"Uh, I'm not sure, but come to think of it, the round, tall ones usually have cherries or crème, and the square ones do seem to have caramel—or jelly."

My friend's eyes were no more than two small slits as she squinted into the box. "Yeah, I read somewhere that the kind of swirl they put on top of the chocolate will tell you what's inside too."

I continued to hold out the box, and she eventually chose a milk chocolate square from the far corner.

"Mmm . . ."

The sound she made reminded me of a contented kitten who had just been given a saucer full of warm milk. I watched as she licked a string of caramel that hung from her lower lip.

"I guess you got your caramel."

Mouth still full, she just smiled.

My friend's indecision reminded me of a well-known character from a popular movie. He commented that life is like a box of chocolates because both hold a wealth of surprises. I see evidence of this all around me but particularly in my three sons. Despite having the same parents and growing up in the same home, each is packed with unique traits.

From the day my oldest son was born, he was a rocket ready to burst into fireworks. His shock of wild blond hair and deep green eyes should have been a giveaway, but his "I'm so innocent" smile fooled me at first. JC (short for John Christopher) always reminded me of a coconut-filled bonbon. You don't get too many of them, and they can catch you off guard.

My middle child is stocky, with curly brown hair. His eyes are blue, but they hold flecks of green and bits of brown that look like chocolate haystacks. He is the typical football lineman—strong and steady. His mind is as brilliant as his will is stubborn. Alan makes me think of a dark chocolate caramel, the kind you'd get in a heart-shaped box for Valentine's Day. It takes a while to get to the center of him, but, oh, the reward you get when you do!

Tim is my youngest. He's six foot four and has straight, dark hair, a most handsome dark complexion, and eyes the color of chestnuts. He is as different from his oldest brother as night is from day. This gifted musician has a very sensitive nature and, despite the rich brown of his eyes, he definitely reflects the character of a white chocolate truffle. He is highbrow and classic all the way.

I love each of my children deeply, but I raised them with a distinctly different hand. You don't bite into a chocolate cordial the same way you crunch on a chocolate-covered nougat! Figuring out what filling was inside my guys wasn't easy, but it was necessary to make the most of their natural talents.

Raising children is certainly more serious than choosing a chocolate. Difficulties appear regularly, and parents often struggle with how to handle these situations. During my parent-child struggles, I would ask for the Creator's help. God would patiently point out the complex ingredients that formed that particular son's personality. When the soft center or the hard nougat inside my boy was revealed, I could apply just the right amount of pressure to release a positive result. The outcome? Three godly young men emerged from rebellious boys.

> If any of you is lacking in wisdom, ask God, who gives to all generously and ungrudgingly, and it will be given you.
>
> James 1:5

Cocoa Quote

All I really need is love, but a little chocolate now and then doesn't hurt!

Lucy Van Pelt (in *Peanuts,* by Charles M. Schulz)

3

Truffles

The gift in my lap was wrapped in brilliant white paper that sparkled with blue and silver stars. After a morning of watching our children open their Christmas gifts, the now familiar sound as I tore the paper from its package seemed an appropriate prelude to the excitement I knew the gift would bring. A smile spread wide across my face as a box of chocolates revealed itself. Early in our marriage my husband figured out the way to my heart. There are always chocolate truffles under the Christmas tree.

I opened the box, offered a sweet to each family member, and then chose a dark chocolate for myself. Its rich outer coating sent joy to my taste buds. But it isn't the outside layer that makes these particular chocolates so special. When the coating gives way to the soft inner core, I close my eyes and sigh. Its rich hazelnut flavor sweeps over me.

Truffles are such a delight. Their flavor makes my heart sing and my spirit dance. When that initial burst of dark sweetness disappears, I know I will take even greater pleasure in what comes next.

I've seen people pop chocolate truffles into their mouths and dispose of them like popcorn at a bad movie. What a waste! They may get that flavor burst, but they never really experience the delicacy inside.

It reminds me of another Christmas gift I received many years ago—a beautifully illustrated copy of the Proverbs of Solomon. When I read the Proverbs, I like to think of them as truffles. Each verse is wonderfully rich when first read, but it seems a shame to summarily dispose of something so delicious. I dwell on every passage for a moment, allowing myself to get past the surface and down to its core, to the significance of the words. The insight revealed when I quickly read through a passage is nothing compared to the substance God imparts when I meditate on his Word.

Whether it's enjoying time with friends, savoring a delicate chocolate truffle, or reading a proverb from God's Word, taking time to savor the occasion always enriches the experience.

How much better to get wisdom than gold! To get understanding is to be chosen rather than silver.

Proverbs 16:16

Fun Fact

The ancient Aztecs were the first known people to consume chocolate. They drank large quantities of "chocolatl," a drink they considered given to them by the gods. The first European visitors described chocolate as "finely ground, soft, foamy, reddish, and bitter." It was combined with chili powder, water, aromatic flowers, vanilla, and wild bee honey. Today we would find it less than palatable, or strangely spicy at best. It bore little resemblance to the hot cocoa we know today.

4

The Day Trip

In my part of the country, any precipitation falling a few days before Christmas is supposed to be snow. But this December 20 as my husband's chipper voice called to me from down the hall, a bleak, rainy sky mocked my new snowflake-strewn sweater.

"You almost ready?" he asked.

"Yeah, I'm coming," I called back, quickly fastening a pair of silver snowflakes to my ears in defiance of the weather.

"Wish this were snow," I grumbled as I stepped out our front door.

"Cheer up. I think the rain is supposed to clear up soon. Um . . . are the umbrellas in the car . . . just in case?" My husband's reluctance to remove the hint of cheer he'd seen flicker across my face was obvious.

I simply nodded. Months before, I had envisioned a wonderful crisp winter day for this outing. I had imagined we would spend the afternoon shopping in quaint shops and top off the evening with an elegant theater production of Charles Dickens's *A Christmas Carol*. Perhaps a few snowflakes would fall just as the moon rose into the starlit night.

This fanciful image had so inspired me that when my son's school offered tickets for this event, I purchased enough for our whole family. What I'd failed to anticipate was the possibility of unseasonable weather.

As we stepped off the tour bus, I put on a brave face and held my umbrella ready.

"Look, the rain's stopped," my husband encouraged, disregarding the fine mist that still hung in the air.

"Almost," I mumbled and opened my protection in protest.

"Come on. You don't need that." He took the umbrella out of my hand and closed it.

Unable to suck him into my puddle of disappointment, I turned to my son and his girlfriend. After we agreed to meet for dinner before the Christmas show, they headed down the street, oblivious to both the unusually warm weather and my displeasure with it.

My husband and I ventured in the opposite direction, where we browsed the festive shop windows and strolled the streets decked in holiday finery. A cute chocolate boutique enticed us to its door, and we entered ready to abandon ourselves to its delectable merchandise. Glass shelves sparkled with red and gold Christmas balls interspersed with platters of delicious chocolates. Each selection I made seemed better than the last, and the small bag I finally clutched at the store's checkout crinkled joyfully to echo my pleasure. As we left the sweet smell of the shop, I was delighted to note that the air was now crisp and the sky was filled with stars. There wasn't so much as a hint of rain. My spirits rose with the falling temperature. We continued to shop, forgetting the umbrellas we'd crammed into our overstuffed shopping bags. By the time we arrived for dinner, the twinkle of the Christmas lights adorning the restaurant window matched the twinkle in my eyes.

Our plans hadn't changed, but our environment certainly seemed sweeter. As my husband and I sipped our white chocolate cappuccinos, I felt ashamed. Circumstances shouldn't affect how a Christian reacts to God's world. Our loving Father blesses those who believe in him and those who don't, and the world's sin touches righteous people as well as the unrighteous. Who was I to think he should order the weather to suit my taste?

The corners of my mouth turned up as I watched my husband sip his gourmet coffee. As usual, our circumstances hadn't flustered my ever-optimistic husband.

"I think we might even get some snow." He smiled back encouragingly.

"I think you might just be right," I replied. No longer bound by the weather, I allowed my smile to fill my soul as well as my face.

> Give thanks in all circumstances; for this is the will of God in Christ Jesus for you.
>
> 1 Thessalonians 5:18

Fun Fact

Hershey's slogan is "Put a smile on your face, make the world a better place."

5

Spoiled

When the email arrived with a frowning alternative to the familiar smiley face, I suspected it would not contain good news.

"We waited too long to eat the chocolates. They spoiled," it read.

Oh no! Could it be that a box of wonderful chocolates had gone to waste? My son and his wife had received a gift box of very fine chocolate cordials. When they told me the name of the chocolatier, I recognized these to be some of the best the world had to offer. Why would they allow such a splendid treat to spoil? Whatever the reason, I knew it couldn't have been intentional.

Having relished the first few pieces, my son and his wife wanted to make their treat last. They're both "savers." I'm sure you know people like this. Savers push their favorite part of a meal to the side of the plate with the intention of saving the best for last. This means they may eat mashed potatoes with cold gravy or follow their pie with ice cream that is more cream than ice.

Now, I'm not saying this is all bad. My son and daughter-in-law put off a few temporary pleasures in order to set aside a house down payment. That certainly was to their advantage.

But not everything should be put off or saved for later. Each of the delicate confections they received was filled with a fine flavored liquid. These chocolates were meant to be appreciated at the time of their arrival. Unlike aged cheese or an exceptional wine, time was their surest enemy. The temperature in the warm apartment quickly evaporated the moist filling and left only an unappetizing glob of crystallized sugar.

I've found that God is pleased when we use our experience to prepare for both expected and unexpected needs. God wants us, like the industrious ant in Aesop's fables, to take advantage of his generosity and anticipate leaner times. But the Scriptures are pretty clear that God doesn't want us to hoard his gifts. Here are some things I've discovered:

- *God's gifts were meant to be used*—When we enjoy his generosity it gives the Lord great pleasure (Eccles. 3:13).
- *God wants us to share his gifts*—In sharing God's bounty, we often experience the pleasure twofold: once when we accept the gift and a second time when we see the joy it gives to someone else (1 Tim. 6:18).
- *God loves us, and he wants us to know it*—Each time we receive a gift from God, we are reminded how much he cares (Ps. 23:1).

No gift from God, large or small, should be hidden away and left to spoil.

> You will be enriched in every way for your great generosity, which will produce thanksgiving to God through us.
>
> 2 Corinthians 9:11

Fun Fact

Seen on a woman's T-shirt: "EMERGENCY ALERT: If wearer of this shirt is found vacant, listless, or depressed, ADMINISTER CHOCOLATE IMMEDIATELY."

6
Salty Sweet

I snuggled down in the chair, tucking the warm blanket around my body. A classic thriller lay open in my lap, and to my right sat one of my favorite sweet treats, a small dish of chocolate-covered pretzels. The salty and sweet flavors are, in my opinion, a perfect complement to each other. My brain does a double dance of satisfaction when these taste buds kick in simultaneously.

That evening I set aside my book and decided to call my sister at her bakery. Separated by hundreds of miles, we make a point of keeping in touch by phone as often as possible. These less-than-personal visits do not, however, allow me to partake of the many wonderful creations she conjures up in her Amazing Cakes bakery.

"Hi, Gretel. What are you up to today?" I didn't attempt to strain the expectancy from my voice. Many of our conversations take place while she's busy molding gum-paste flowers, pouring fondant, or baking some glorious confection. Hearing her describe her magnificent creations is the next best thing to being there.

"I'm getting ready to dip pretzels."

"Dip pretzels?" I asked, my sweet tooth aching with pleasure at the thought. "You aren't going to believe this, but I'm eating chocolate-covered pretzels right now!"

"Really," she answered, obviously unimpressed. "I'm making them for a baby shower. I use the large rods, not the little knot-shaped ones. First I dip the end in caramel, and then I dip it in chocolate. When they dry I slip each into a cellophane sleeve and tie it with a pretty ribbon."

I felt my eyes bug out like a cartoon character slammed with a mallet. My distress leached into my voice. "Why on earth would you want to do that?"

I heard the usual rustle of her work stop momentarily as confusion took its place. "What are you talking about?" she asked.

"What am I talking about? You have a perfectly delicious pretzel and a pot of soul-satisfying chocolate. What more do you need? Why ruin that wonderful combination by dipping the pretzel in caramel first?"

"Because the caramel cuts the salt," she responded with matter-of-fact logic.

"But why would you want to do that?"

"I think that's obvious!"

My poor sister then had to listen to my tirade of how the salt and sweet were meant for each other. After some considerable discussion, we parted without my persuasive powers winning out. Gretel doesn't like the taste of salt with sweet, and by now I think it's clear that I do.

This whole unsettling exchange reminded me of a conversation I had with a co-worker of mine. We were discussing the differences in our church services. She attends a liturgical church. They hold a somewhat formal service where the priests wear robes, the order of the service is set by the church hierarchy, and the people accept the decisions made by those who rule their denomination. I belong to a congregational church. Our minister wears a suit and tie, the service is less formal, and decisions are made by vote.

What does this have to do with chocolate-covered pretzels? Well, it finally occurred to me that it doesn't really matter how we serve up our chocolate-covered pretzels. Even if my sister adds caramel to suit her taste, her treat still starts with the same pretzel and ends with it being covered in chocolate.

Jesus Christ should be the foundation of our Christian faith no matter what our form of worship. Individuals may exhibit reverence by kneeling or by dancing. Voices may accompany electric guitars, a cathedral's organ, or nothing at all. Differences in mannerisms and personality are not issues of faith. They are simply evidence that our Lord is the grand master of variety.

> For no one can lay any foundation other than the one that has been laid; that foundation is Jesus Christ.
>
> 1 Corinthians 3:11

Cocoa Quote

Milton Hershey, the founder of the famous Hershey chocolate empire, started out making caramels. Once he discovered chocolate, however, he sold his caramel business and devoted himself solely to his new love.

Caramels are only a fad. Chocolate is a permanent thing.

Milton Snavely Hershey

7

Sunrise Baking

I heard the incessant buzzing of the alarm but chose to roll over instead of rising to its call. My husband's bare feet made a soft pitter-patter sound on the wood floor as he strode to our dresser and silenced the alarm's relentless plea for attention. Refusing to get out of bed, I burrowed deeper into the warm cocoon I'd entered the evening before. I was taking the day off from work—for me there would be no rushing headlong into the black morning and no scraping frost off car windows.

I moved not a muscle as I heard the shower shut off. Feigning sleep, I listened as John quietly dressed using only the dim light from our master bath. I knew I should get up. I had dozens and dozens of fancy cookies to make. But a peculiar thought began to hack its nasty little way into my consciousness. If I chose to make simple cookies, I would be done in about half the time. No one expected me to make the elegant bittersweet-chocolate-dipped, almond-rolled, sugar-sprinkled confections I had planned. Keeping it simple would allow me to sleep late.

John fumbled for his keys on the nightstand, then leaned over and planted a kiss on my cheek.

"You told me to wake you before I left. Are you getting up, or should I reset the alarm to give you another hour of sleep?" Through the squint of one eye, I saw him grin unmercifully as he jostled the covers once again. I deliberately squeezed my eyes shut and refused to reply.

"OK, then. I'm leaving now. Have fun baking," he called over his shoulder.

"Sure thing," I mumbled in return.

The front door thumped closed a moment later. I rolled over, punched the pillow, and sought a cozy position that would let sleep return, but God wouldn't allow me to rest.

"It's only 5:45 a.m.," I grumbled. "I have a right to sleep in this once."

Silence surrounded me like water envelops a drowning man. God had my attention. I washed, dressed, and brewed a large pot of coffee. Sipping my first cup, I watched the early rays of morning stream through the front window.

"Awesome, God," I whispered. "Thanks."

Getting up early to bake and chocolate-coat twenty dozen cookies wasn't such a big deal. Each morning, my heavenly Father generously creates for me a brand-new sunrise. For my pleasure he laces each spring with the fragrance of flowers, and in the winter he coats my bleak, sin-dusted world with fresh, white snow.

I could have prepared a quick bar cookie recipe, but God was calling me to put myself into my gift. This wasn't about making cookies for a group of senior citizens. My task was to prepare sweets that would share Christ with men and women who needed to feel the kiss of his sunrise. Refreshed by God's presence, I eagerly picked up a bag of chocolate chips and turned toward my oven. It was time to get to work.

> Now concerning love of the brothers and sisters, you do not need to have anyone write to you, for you yourselves have been taught by

God to love one another; and indeed you do. . . . But we urge you, beloved, to do so more and more, to aspire to live quietly, to mind your own affairs, and to work with your hands, as we directed you, so that you may behave properly toward outsiders.

1 Thessalonians 4:9–12

Fun Fact

Baby Ruth candy bars are named not for the famous home run king but for President Grover Cleveland's youngest daughter, Ruth.

8

Accountability

I felt as if a Boy Scout were practicing tying knots in my stomach. No matter how I tried, I couldn't get my mind off my friend's phone call, and now my head ached to boot. A hot blush of remembered shame crept up my neck each time the phone rang. How could I have let my friend down like this?

My teenager had been looking for a part-time job. He needed the extra cash, but his school schedule and a long list of extracurricular activities prevented him from finding suitable work. His financial frustrations were reaching a peak at about the same time my good friend asked me for a favor. She wanted me to look after her house and her cats for a few weeks, and I was glad to help out. About a week into her trip I came down with the flu. It occurred to me that perhaps my son could do this chore for some extra money. He and I agreed that it would fit into his schedule, and I offered to pay him for the job.

The problem was that he forgot to take care of one detail. He had the brilliant idea to soak the cat food cans in the sink before taking them to the recycling center. Before he had the chance to rinse them, we had a snowstorm and he got busy shoveling the driveways. Being a teenager with the attention span of a two-year-old, he forgot all about the cans. The result left my friend with quite a mess and a very smelly house. Why was I embarrassed? Because I knew I'd let her down. I was the one who had agreed to care for her house and her cats. True, my son did tell me he would do the job, but it was still my duty to make sure the job got done right. I had a lot of reasons why I didn't do a final check on the house. We had two snowstorms while my friend was away, and there was that pesky flu. Did that relieve me of my accountability? I don't think so. It may explain why I didn't get over to her house for a quick inspection the day before her return, but it doesn't change the fact that I'm responsible for my actions as well as those of my son.

We all encounter circumstances that leave us looking for an excuse. Holiday celebrations and birthday parties ruin many diets. "It's not my fault!" you hear the weight watcher cry. "My sister knew I was on a diet, and she still made her chocolate trifle. How can I pass up my favorite dessert?"

We can trace blaming others all the way back to the Garden of Eden. When God confronted Adam, Adam blamed Eve for giving him the fruit in the first place. When God spoke to Eve, she told him the serpent had tricked her into eating the fruit. Both statements were true, but only in part.

The whole truth is that we have the right to make both good and bad choices. When chocolate trifle is passed around the table, I can quietly pass it on, politely take only a small portion, or load my plate high and deal with the calories. When my friend asks a favor, I can do the job myself, make sure someone else does the job correctly, or take the blame when something goes wrong.

I'm not sure what I can do to make up for my mistake in judgment. I apologized and my son apologized, yet things don't feel right between us. I have no doubt that my gracious friend has already forgiven me, but that doesn't change the hurt and disappointment she felt, nor does it relieve me of the consequences that come with my neglect.

God knew the devastation of sin. He saw that even one little mistake would so taint our lives that nothing we could do would fix it. Rather than have us sit with knotted stomachs, twisting hands, and aching heads, God provided a once-and-for-all solution—the sacrifice of his Son. We must still be accountable for our actions, but now when we mess up, God is able to see past the mistake to the one who paid the price and cleaned up our mess.

> For whoever keeps the whole law but fails in one point has become accountable for all of it.
>
> James 2:10

Fun Fact

The white film that appears on chocolate after exposure to different temperatures won't affect the taste or the quality of the chocolate.

9

Instant Disaster

Leslie smiled as she measured her ingredients into a rainbow of small glass bowls. The dishes were a wedding gift from her sister, who was a gourmet cook of some note. She ran her finger around the smooth glass rim of a bowl the color of pure turquoise. Just touching its cool surface gave Leslie confidence in her cooking ability. Squaring her shoulders, Leslie removed a set of russet-colored ramekins from her cupboard and placed them to the side of her stove.

She and her husband, Joe, were newlyweds, and this was Leslie's first attempt at a dinner party. The set of her jaw clearly illustrated her determination. Everything had to be perfect. A prime rib roast simmered amid red potatoes and savory vegetables, while a cleverly arranged antipasto chilled in the fridge. All that remained to be done was the chocolate custard dessert.

With a hint of steam rising from the edge of the double boiler, Leslie began combining the ingredients her cookbook listed. Sugar, shaved chocolate, and heavy cream were carefully heated until the mixture swirled into luscious chocolate ribbons. She whisked the egg yolks in the turquoise bowl. This was the tricky part according to the recipe. If you add the yolks too fast, the eggs could scramble and ruin the custard.

Leslie took a deep breath. With her left hand she poured a small amount of the eggs into the warm mixture. With her right hand she worked the whisk, incorporating the yolks into the sugar, cream, and chocolate. The corners of her mouth turned upward slightly. The mixture was blending beautifully. She poured in a bit more yolk and whisked again. Her smile broadened as her confidence soared. Clearly this was not as hard as the cookbook implied. Leslie glanced at the clock. If she hurried this along just a bit, she would have time to unpack and wash the beautiful lead crystal napkin rings Aunt Alice had given them. It would add the perfect touch to this special dinner. Leslie poured the remainder of the eggs into the warm pot just as the phone rang.

"Hi, Leslie! Tim and I are looking forward to coming tonight. Anything we can bring?"

"No. I've got everything under control."

Leslie had only turned her back on the stove for a moment. From behind her she now heard a strangled gasp as the custard overheated. Dropping the phone, Leslie dashed for the stove and began madly whisking the contents of the double boiler.

"Leslie? Leslie, are you there?" her friend called from the dangling phone.

With a huge sigh Leslie removed the pot from the burner, turned off the stove, and returned to the phone.

"Sorry about that, Carol," she said. "I was making chocolate custard for our dessert, and now it's ruined."

"Really? You were only on the phone for a second. How did that happen?"

"You have to beat egg yolks into a mixture of warm cream and sugar. If you don't keep stirring it or if you pour the eggs in too fast, they don't blend, they cook. Instead of custard I have sweet, creamy, chocolate with scrambled eggs."

"Yuck."

"Hey, you still want to bring something tonight?"

"Sure."

"How about bringing a half gallon of chocolate chunk ice cream for dessert?"

Shortcuts and moments of distraction can take their toll on us all. A ruined dessert can be replaced, but the past has shown me I must be more than vigilant when it comes to matters of faith.

> Therefore, since we are surrounded by so great a cloud of witnesses, let us also lay aside every weight and the sin that clings so closely, and let us run with perseverance the race that is set before us.
>
> Hebrews 12:1

Fun Fact

When baking you can often substitute one type of baking chocolate for another. You can use three level tablespoons of unsweetened cocoa powder plus one tablespoon of vegetable shortening *or* one square (one ounce) of unsweetened baking chocolate *or* one envelope (one ounce) of pre-melted unsweetened chocolate.

10

Chocolate Chip Blessings

"If you want to have chocolate chips in these cookies, you'd better get your fingers out of that bag," I calmly instructed my son.

"I know you always buy a second bag of chips when you make these," he said, grinning as he popped the last of the pilfered chips into his mouth.

I turned a cup of packed brown sugar into the bowl in front of me and started the mixer. Pretty paisley swirls formed as the butter met the white and brown sugars before I responded.

"That may be, but there still won't be enough if you keep eating them. I'm going to make a second batch of cookies today. The first is for the school concert refreshments. The second batch is for us. Keep popping them in your mouth, and I'll only have enough to put in the school's cookies. Ours will be plain drop cookies—without chips."

My son's eyebrows rose as fast as his hand fell away from the open bag of chocolate.

"What good are chocolate chip cookies without chocolate chips?" he grumbled.

"Good question. I guess you'd better leave them alone." I threw him a less than sympathetic smile, then cracked the eggs into the batter and scraped the sides of the bowl.

My son's eyes brightened as he sent me one of his chipmunklike, dimpled smiles.

"If I eat the chips now, all I'll get is a handful of chocolate. If I wait, I'll still get the chips—only then the chips will be surrounded by cookie!"

My face broke out in a smile as I acknowledged his logic. "I guess that could make it worth waiting for."

While the cookies baked I thought about the wisdom exhibited by my young son. In this day of fast food and instant coffee, too many of us refuse the lesson of patience. The media convinces young adults that love in physical form is theirs for the taking. A dinner or a few drinks is the customary price. Waiting for the marriage bed seems hardly worth the invested time.

Middle-income men and women look for a quick fix to their financial problems. Buy now, pay later plans have taken their toll. We run to consolidate our debt only to max out our credit cards once again with the purchase of more gadgets and goodies.

Senior citizens who for years struggled for each dollar now throw their savings into the market's latest dot-com, hoping for a windfall profit at the cusp of their golden years.

The world throws confetti, waves banners, and shrieks, "Grab what you can. You deserve only the best. Take it now!"

God quietly whispers, "Wait. Don't settle for secondhand goods. I have something of real value—learn patience."

Waiting isn't easy, but there are incentives. I've experienced the pleasure of snuggling down in my favorite chair with a large, freshly baked chocolate chip cookie and a hot cup of coffee. Wolfing down a handful of cold chocolate chips just can't compare to that.

> Happy is the one who listens to me, watching daily at my gates, waiting beside my doors.
>
> Proverbs 8:34

Fun Fact

The first chocolate chips were introduced by Nestlé in the year 1939. For your eating pleasure they now produce approximately 250 million chips per day. Each twelve-ounce bag contains around 675 chocolate chips.

11

Chocolate Eyes

I love the color of my husband's eyes. The color is rich and even, like pools of dark melted chocolate. My eyes are green—sort of. It all depends on what I wear. I've worn deep shades of turquoise that made them look blue. And when I wear gold, they turn the strangest sort of gray. I don't much like the color of my eyes. If they have to be green, why can't they be emerald green—a jewel-like green that sparkles in the sunshine and flashes fire when filled with passion? Instead, my capricious color changes to accommodate its surroundings.

My husband is as steady as the rich color of his eyes—always ready with a hand to help, not quick to anger or overly quick with unwanted advice. Sure and steady, just like his beautiful brown eyes.

With some thought, I find that I may, sadly, be more like my changeable eyes than I would like. There are times I want to grab my spoken words out of the air and stuff them back down my throat. I want to shout, "I have a right to do what I want to do," and my attitude depends on nothing more than changing circumstances. If conditions fall to my advantage, I snatch the opportunity to gain ground. Like my eyes, my approach reflects what is around me. When I'm with those of affluence and authority, it's easy to forget that my perceived good looks, brilliant wit, and sparkling personality haven't earned me the good things that have fallen into my lap. When I'm with those who grumble, I readily find reasons for my own discontent.

God doesn't call us to be tossed about by our circumstances, and he doesn't want our color to change with every encounter. He offers hope to those who have chameleon tendencies. We can sit firmly on the Rock of Ages and allow our personalities to permanently reflect the color of our Lord. When we remain in Christ, we consistently reflect the one who is and was and will be for all time.

I still love my dear husband's beautiful, chocolate brown eyes more than my capricious green ones, but the stability of my foundation, not the fickle color of my eyes, is what counts.

> So then, brothers and sisters, stand firm and hold fast to the traditions that you were taught by us, either by word of mouth or by our letter.
>
> 2 Thessalonians 2:15

Cocoa Quote

What you see before you, my friend, is the result of a lifetime of chocolate.

Katharine Hepburn

12

Satisfaction

With great care I unwrapped the pretty green foil that covered my treasure. Even through the wrapping I could smell the invigorating scent of mint and the intense sweetness of the chocolate. I popped the imported chocolate into my mouth and let it melt slowly, savoring the rich flavor.

One of chocolate's many beneficial qualities is brought forward when it is combined with mint. Scientific studies prove that mint wakes you up and makes you more productive. Join mint and chocolate, and you have a particularly good afternoon pick-me-up. Even the small amount of caffeine and sugar that comes in a little Hershey's Kiss can't but help you through a rough afternoon.

So I allowed the taste, smell, and luscious flavor of that bit of delight to infuse every inch of my being. But the moment was fleeting. In less time than it would take to say, "I'd like a Chunky Monkey and chocolate chip double-dip cone, please," the pleasure was gone.

The refreshment of this world is like that. You take a nice cool dip in the pool, but five minutes after you dry off, the sun resumes its relentless persistence, and you have to dive back in for more. Remember the day you finished that huge Thanksgiving dinner and topped it off with pecan pie? You had two cups of coffee while you tried to digest the lot of it. Your straining slacks begged you to resume your diet, but the next afternoon you dived right into a double-decker turkey and stuffing sandwich. Such are the ways of this world.

The author of the book of Ecclesiastes knew all about dissatisfaction. Like many today, he wanted the secret to happiness and contentment. He felt that mastering numerous academic disciplines would achieve this goal, but after years of work he concluded that wisdom brings with it great sorrow. Then he thought that perhaps physical pleasure would be the key to happiness. He ate gourmet foods, drank only the finest wines, and loved many women. These temporary pleasures felt wonderful, but they did not satisfy his deeper needs, and their bliss was fleeting. He sought something that would last. So he turned to grand building projects to find contentment. Stately houses with every modern convenience rose to the heavens. Vast vineyards spread across the hillsides. He purchased herds of fine livestock; amassed a huge fortune of gold, silver, and other treasures; and kept a harem larger than any other man's. He surrounded himself with beautiful art and music, then acquired great political power.

Surely, he thought, *with all of this, I cannot run out of happiness!*

But at the end of his pursuit, his conclusion was this: "And what I toiled to achieve, everything was meaningless, a chasing after the wind; nothing was gained under the sun" (Eccles. 2:11 NIV).

Just like the mint and the chocolate, life for the writer of Ecclesiastes tasted good for only a short while. His achievements refreshed for a brief moment.

All this may seem pretty depressing, but take heart; I've found that God is not a God of despair but a God of hope! When we are done running around, trying to find things that will keep us happy, we conclude that there is only one thing that works—one thing that satisfies. Jesus. Are you done chasing the wind?

> And my God will fully satisfy every need of yours according to his riches in glory in Christ Jesus.
>
> Philippians 4:19

Sweet Poetry

Chocolate Haiku

My daughters and I
stash bittersweet in our desks
One bonbon at two

Maude Carolan

13

The Cure

The sign on the door read, "Chocolate—the Cure for What Ails You."

"I can agree to that!" my friend chirped as we entered the Chocolate Boutique.

"No argument here," I said as we entered. I breathed in the delectable fragrance of chocolate.

We ogled the glossy confections, tasted sweet samples, and shopped our way around the little store. Each item seemed more desirable than the next. One corner was dedicated to coffee-related items. There were chocolate-covered spoons to flavor your coffee, mocha mixes containing careful blends of coffee and dark chocolate, and chocolate-laced cookies created especially to enhance a cup of good java. This was my idea of an earthly paradise.

My friend's arms were laden with goodies, and I balanced my own load precariously as we continued to shop.

"We have to get out of here soon, or we'll have to take out a second mortgage to pay the bill," I said with a laugh, catching a slipping bag of truffles with my pinky.

She smiled but didn't look up from a display of beautifully crafted chocolate lollipops.

"I'm trying to find just a few more things to put into my kids' college care packages. When exam time comes around, I always send a package of snacks, goodies, and school supplies. I try to put in things they can't or won't buy for themselves. Some of this stuff is just so cute. I know they'll love it."

"So chocolate is your cure for the college exam blues?" I asked.

She chuckled. "To some extent you're right. But what I think the kids appreciate even more than the chocolate is the fact that I go out of my way to find special treats."

She held up a white ceramic kitten with a pink velvet ribbon draped lazily around its neck. Between the animal's front paws sat a tulle bag of dainty chocolate truffles. "This is for my daughter. In her last email she told me how much she misses our cat. She got Puffin when he was only six weeks old. He's seventeen now, and my daughter is worried that he won't be around when she finishes college. Maybe this will cheer her up a little."

Next she held up a bag of white-chocolate-covered popcorn. The bag was emblazoned with a local hockey team's emblem. Tucked alongside was a commemorative schedule of their games and miniature puck. "This is for my son. Because he's going to school out of state, he misses hanging out with all his friends and watching the local games. He loves his college, but the schools down south aren't really into ice hockey. Somehow, I think he'll enjoy this popcorn more because of the hockey items that come with it."

I looked down at my own stash of treats. White-chocolate-covered key lime cookies for my husband, two peanut-butter-and-chocolate-covered pretzel sticks for my youngest son, and a single cappuccino-flavored truffle for my other son. I'd certainly found some pick-me-ups for each of my crew.

As nice as these gifts were, I couldn't help but feel just a bit uncomfortable with the sign that once again caught my eye as I left the store. It seems that our offerings would certainly bring a smile to the lips of those receiving them, but could chocolate really cure what ails the world?

Imagine for a moment. Poverty, plagues, heartache—all cured with a cup of hot cocoa. War on the eastern front? Send a few Snickers bars. Envy in the west? Hershey's to the rescue. If only it were that easy. Chocolate at its best is only a momentary vacation from our troubles. For the real cure, I've found a more permanent solution.

> Heal me, O Lord, and I shall be healed; save me, and I shall be saved; for you are my praise.
>
> Jeremiah 17:4

Cocoa Quote

Strength is the capacity to break a chocolate bar into four pieces with your bare hands—and then eat just one of the pieces.

Judith Viorst

14

Lattice and Leaves

The young boy stood with wide eyes, staring at the rich chocolate icing on the cake before him.

"Chocolate leaves? Do they grow on chocolate trees?" he asked in a small, awe-filled voice.

"Those aren't real leaves, honey. The baker makes the chocolate look like leaves. You can eat them just like a chocolate Easter bunny," his mother said.

"They look so real," he said, almost whispering.

I couldn't help but nod in agreement. The sugar-coated marzipan fruit glistened as if coated with tiny drops of dew, and the fragile chocolate leaves left the impression that they could be swept away with a light evening breeze. Along the side of the cake ran a latticework trellis made of chocolate. Its beauty made me want to hold my breath.

"Hard to believe this is just a cake, isn't it?" I said to the woman who gently held back the small child's curious fingers.

She responded, shaking her head, "It's a lot more than a cake. It's a work of art."

Attending a chocolate fair is always a delight for me. Masterful sketches airbrushed in varying shades of liquid chocolate, delicately shaved chocolate and candy curls floating atop clouds of frosting, and finely spun nests of glistening sugar are just a few of the offerings. Each creation seems more intricate than the last. Passersby ooh and ah at the handiwork and wonder at each chef's mastery and craftsmanship.

But I have inside information. My sister is a pastry chef, and I know that what you see is not always what you get when it comes to decorating competitions. I used to wonder how they got the buttercream icing to last for hours under those hot lights. I found out from my sister that it doesn't turn rancid because there's no butter in the buttercream! My sister tells me the rules differ with each competition but most only insist that entries are constructed in such a way that they *could* be made entirely edible. For display purposes, they often use Styrofoam bases in place of cake and icing without butterfat. Everything looks beautiful, but underneath the sparkle and shine there is little substance.

The line between illusion and deception blurs. Those who enter a decorating competition know the rules. The judges look for artistry, technique, and originality; they are not expecting dessert.

When a person is led to believe that something is what it is not, deception takes place. Satan is called the father of lies and the great deceiver. He likes to hide in shadows and cloaks himself with half-truths. God, on the other hand, is called the Father of lights. You will not find illusion in his work. God may do things we don't understand, but everything he does is real, not illusion.

In these days when special effects and scam artists make the counterfeit seem all too real, it is nice to know that there is still one thing in which I can trust without hesitation—my Father in heaven.

> Do not be deceived, my beloved. . . . every perfect gift, is from above, coming down from the Father of lights, with whom there is no variation or shadow due to change.
>
> James 1:16–17

Pleasant Pastime

Kissy Mice

Materials needed to make two mice

¼ yard of half-inch pink grosgrain ribbon
1 sheet of pink felt
4 jiggly craft eyes
4 candy kisses
low-heat hot glue
scissors

Instructions

Tails—Cut two 2-inch lengths of thin, pink grosgrain ribbon. Pinch one end of each ribbon in half and glue the pinched end onto the pointy side of two candy kisses.

Ears—Trace a dime onto the pink felt four times. Cut these four mouselike ears out of the pink felt. Lay one kiss, with a tail, on its side. Glue a small section of two ears to the flat side of the kiss. Glue the other two ears to the second kiss that has a tail. This will leave two curve shapes extending over the edge to form the ears.

Body—Glue the flat sides of the two remaining kisses to the flat sides of the kisses that have the ears and the tails. The felt ears should nest between the kisses.

Eyes—Finish the mice by gluing two jiggly eyes onto the kisses that do not have the tails.

51

15

Mac and Cheese

Imagine rolled rib roasts stuffed with homemade cornbread and plump portabella mushrooms or paella brimming with fresh mussels and lobster claws. These are just two of the delightful dishes my husband prepared last year. John is not a chef. He only began cooking when I reentered the workforce, but he quickly acquired the ability to know what a dish needs. He takes a small taste and then remarks, "Hmm, this needs a bit more thyme."

I, on the other hand, have trouble cooking macaroni and cheese out of one of those blue and gold boxes. There are times when measuring the milk and cutting just the right amount of butter off the stick seems like more trouble than it's worth. When my oldest son went away to college, I noticed an even easier version of this convenience product. All you need for the new version is water, a microwave, and the package of macaroni and cheese. But something gets lost in the quick and easy process when you don't make macaroni and cheese from scratch.

My friend made homemade macaroni and cheese for her kids the other day. She baked it in a beautiful amber-glass pan and covered it with cheddar that toasted to a crispy crust. It tasted nothing like the boxed version. My sister makes a homemade chocolate cake that puts every commercial cake mix to shame. What is it about the shortcut that changes the dishes' texture and richness? As corny as it may sound, both my sister and my friend might say it was love that made their dishes so appetizing.

Sometimes love and the giving of our time are one and the same. We all know it takes just minutes to whip up a chocolate cake mix. I always have a few boxes of this staple handy in my pantry. The extras—water, eggs, and butter—are also readily available at my house. If you prepare the from-scratch version of this cake, you first have to do some planning. You need good baking chocolate, fresh baking powder, and a variety of other ingredients. When you prepare the cake you must be vigilant about stirring the chocolate as it melts. Every hint of moisture must be kept out of the chocolate lest it seize. Then you diligently sift the flour with the other elements and carefully measure the remaining ingredients. This takes more time than tossing a mix into the bowl and adding water.

Everyone is in a hurry these days. We have more labor-saving devices, and we perform fewer manual tasks. But making extra effort can be a gift in and of itself. What father does not treasure the handmade card created by his ten-year-old daughter? What mother does not shed a tear of joy when presented with handpicked dandelions stuffed into a paper-cone vase?

These gifts are precious not because of their monetary value but because of the love they represent. Making macaroni and cheese or chocolate cake from scratch feeds not only the recipient's body but also his or her spirit. Not everyone has the talent of a master chef, but we can all offer our best effort.

> I know your works—your love, faith, service, and patient endurance. I know that your last works are greater than the first.
>
> Revelation 2:19

Whatever your task, put yourselves into it, as done for the Lord.

Colossians 3:23

Recipe to Relish

Cheater's Chocolate Sundae

1 cup vanilla or chocolate low-fat frozen yogurt
1 Tbsp. toasted slivered almonds
3 Tbsp. seedless raspberry jam
3 Tbsp. chocolate syrup
mini marshmallows, granola, wheat germ, sprinkles (optional)

Spoon yogurt into a parfait dish, layering it with raspberry jam and/or chocolate syrup. Dress with remaining ingredients. Enjoy.

16

The Need

The tabloid banner caught my eye and drew me in like a good fisherman reels in a fighting trout: "Women Need Chocolate—Scientists Provide Proof." This matter-of-fact, without-apology headline mocked me as I avoided the large assortment of neatly arranged chocolate bars stacked below it. I found myself glaring at the diminutive white-coated scientist on the cover of the newspaper. The broad grin she managed while devouring a contemptuously large chocolate bar seemed to prove her point nicely.

My muscles tensed, and I could feel a seed of desire begin to creep into my mind. If only this could be true. Dare I believe such an outrageous claim? If chocolate had some viable claim on healthful properties, I could indulge myself without guilt.

I glanced anxiously over my shoulder. No one was looking. With all the stealth of a sleight-of-hand master, I slipped a copy of the tabloid facedown onto the counter and pushed other groceries around it. Despite my efforts, I was caught.

"Can you believe that headline? It wouldn't surprise me if the chocolate industry was behind that study," the woman behind me commented.

"Yeah, that's probably where it came from," I said, trying not to blush. Eager to recover, I added, "They do have what looks like a nice recipe for butterscotch brownies in there though."

"Really? That does sound good."

I turned away, busying myself with grocery bags and the bill.

When I got home I unloaded my purchases and once again came across the newspaper. A fresh rush of blood reached my face as I wondered how I could be taken in by their claims.

Pulling up a chair and pouring a fresh cup of coffee, I determined to read this article and put their claims to rest—once and for all.

I was surprised to find that their contentions were not as ridiculous as they first seemed. Chocolate bars contain more than three hundred different constituent compounds. Some, like cocoa butter, make our brains release endorphins. Endorphins produce feelings of pleasure and reduce our susceptibility to pain. In theory, during periods of hormonal stress chocolate could help women cope with life's ups and downs.

The problem is that these facts are skewed. The quantity of chocolate that the average person would need to release enough endorphins for euphoria would be substantial. Even I can't imagine eating that much chocolate without getting sick to my stomach.

People often believe what they want to believe. A teenager may blame his parents for his lack of friends. A wife may excuse her affair because she feels unloved by her husband. Hurt people look for relief at the nearest available source. Cults prey on unhappy individuals and those who feel unloved.

So much of what people say is one part truth twisted with two parts exaggeration. The only one we can count on for the whole truth is God. His words and deeds never tear down, they always lift us up, and they are always intended for our ultimate good.

> And he said, "Beware that you are not led astray; for many will come in my name and say, 'I am he!' and, 'The time is near!' Do not go after them."
>
> Luke 21:8

Cocoa Quote

It's not that chocolates are a substitute for love. Love is a substitute for chocolate. Chocolate is, let's face it, far more reliable than a man.

Miranda Ingram

17

Diets and Dessert

"Check this out! We can have chocolate mousse for dessert."

I peered over the top of my menu and sent an incredulous look in my friend's direction. "Why are you looking at the desserts? You haven't even ordered your meal yet!"

Her calm smile told me this wasn't the first time she had heard this question.

"I always look at the desserts first."

"But that makes no sense. Why tempt yourself with something you can't have even before you start eating?" I asked.

"Who says I can't have it?"

"I know you've been on a diet. Everyone is talking about how great you look!"

"Thanks, but that has nothing to do with my having dessert."

"What?"

"Let's say we order a great meal and we're just sitting here chatting and having a grand old time."

"OK."

"Then the waitress comes back and asks if we want dessert. She just happens to mention that they have chocolate mousse."

"So . . ."

"Are you really going to pass that up?"

"Well . . . maybe, maybe not."

"My point exactly. Wouldn't it be better to know they have chocolate mousse, decide if you want some, and then plan your calorie intake accordingly?"

"I guess, but chocolate mousse can't possibly be on your diet!"

"Look, I can eat anything I want, but it's not always in my best interest to do that. When I'm really hungry I might have a heaping bowl of beef stew and skip dessert. When my sweet tooth starts making me crazy, I cut back on my other calories so I can include a special treat. Sometimes I make dessert a part of the plan, and sometimes I don't."

We both ordered a small chef salad and then split a serving of chocolate mousse. I left that diner both satisfied and encouraged. Maybe I've been going about dieting all wrong. Instead of thinking about what I can't have, I should be thinking about the consequences that result from my choices.

Some people believe God is all about restrictions, but contrary to popular belief, the Ten Commandments (aka "the Thou Shalt Nots") weren't given to spoil our party. They were provided to help us avoid serious negative consequences. We can't eat dish after dish of chocolate mousse without paying a price. Some things are OK in moderation; others should be avoided at all cost. God does not stop us from making choices, but the choices we make do reflect who we are and whom we serve.

> "All things are lawful for me," but not all things are beneficial. "All things are lawful for me," but I will not be dominated by anything.
>
> 1 Corinthians 6:12

Fun Fact

If you are watching your calorie or fat intake, do not substitute diet margarine or low-fat spreads in chocolate recipes that call for butter. Your recipe will not produce acceptable results. Instead, look for chocolate recipes that call for skim milk or low-fat products. Also note that dark chocolate contains fewer calories and less fat than milk chocolate. If you are watching your calories, look for recipes that call for dark chocolate.

18

One Drop

I felt the storm's approach even before it took hold. Dark clouds boiled like a witch's cauldron, and the raw night air reminded me that autumn would soon give way to winter. I left the car running as I waited for my son to get out of work. The heater blasted, but even that couldn't warm my bones. I wrapped my fingers a bit more tightly around the paper coffee cup I held. It wasn't a mocha latte, but the warmth it brought me was enough.

Time dragged, and my mind wandered aimlessly from one thing to the next. Then the rain came. One huge drop splattered my dry windshield and landed right in my line of sight. It seemed to move in slow motion. The moment the raindrop touched the glass, I saw it explode into thousands of tiny diamondlike droplets.

Then another raindrop landed . . . and yet another. Now the rain fell steadily. I could no longer distinguish one drop from the others. The small *plop* made by the first droplet turned into the rhythmic *rat-a-tat* of a snare drum.

I set down my cup and laid my hand against the cold windshield. As soon as the drops hit, they tossed aside their independence and merged with others. Rivulets of water ran down the glass, down the car, and onto the parking lot. My imagination took flight. I imagined the water soaking into the ground beneath me and then into our community wells. I wondered where my raindrop would be in the months to come. Perhaps it would give a newborn baby his first bath at the gentle hands of his mother, or maybe an elderly gentleman would share a moment of comfort with an old friend over a morning cup of coffee brewed with this water. I envisioned a teenager proudly washing the worn paint on his first car and a little girl having a cup of warm cocoa and cookies with her aunt.

Tears stung my eyes. Could one little raindrop do so much? Followed by others I believed it could.

I thought back to the day my second son, Alan, shared his love for Jesus with his little brother. Alan was no more than eight years old when the two of them sat cross-legged on their bedroom floor. Tim was a mere preschooler, but the serious tone of his brother's voice conveyed the importance of Alan's message. Alan was like the first drop. Their conversation didn't make the nightly news, but it mattered greatly in our family—and in God's plan. With one child's message, rivulets began to flow. Dozens, perhaps even hundreds, of others have come to know their Savior through the faith of these young men. As the kids would say—this is *truly awesome!*

The cold rain continued its tune on the roof of my car. One drop at a time, it added to the wealth of wells, rivers, and oceans. Despite the chill, I no longer needed coffee or hot chocolate to warm me—my memories provided warmth from within.

> So deeply do we care for you that we are determined to share with you not only the gospel of God but also our own selves.
>
> 1 Thessalonians 2:8

Cocoa Quote

There's nothing better than a good friend, except a good friend with chocolate.

Linda Grayson

19

$\mathcal{DNA}$ $\mathcal{Giveaway}$

"Oh, come on. I've got no time for this," I muttered, pounding the envelope with the flat of my hand. Despite an abundance of saliva, its flap continued to pop up, mocking every attempt to secure it. I checked my watch. The envelope had to get in the mail that day, and I was already late for work.

"Hey, Timothy. Do you know where my tape dispenser is?"

"It's on the bookshelf," he called from the bathroom, his mouth full of toothpaste.

I hurried to the bookshelf, pulled some tape from the holder, and neatly placed two strips across the resistant flap.

"Perfect." I smiled, grabbing my jacket and bag.

"You find it?" my son asked, coming down the hallway, his toothbrush in hand.

"Yup, thanks," I called, breezing past his strapping, teenage frame. Just as I got to the door, a thought occurred to me, and I turned back to my son.

"Hey, why are you carrying your toothbrush into the living room?"

"It's the anniversary of the discovery of the DNA helix. We're bringing in things that have our DNA on it. Hey, don't leave without your mail . . . and your lunch."

"Oops." I retraced my steps, stuffed the envelope into the side pouch of my purse, and grabbed the brown bag my son held out. "Thanks again. See you later."

As I trotted down our front walk, the wind tugged at the envelope. Its white surface fluttered in the stiff breeze, and the morning sun poured its light onto the cellophane tape. That is when I saw the smudge. Right under the cellophane tape I could detect the faintest outline of a chocolate fingerprint, evidence of the lunch I'd prepared earlier. I hurriedly popped the letter into my mailbox, but the image would not leave my brain.

My saliva's DNA was mixed with the minty tasting gum on the flap, and my chocolate fingerprints were plastered all over the cellophane tape. Evidence of my presence screamed out to anyone who would listen. Visions of forensic scientists bent over the envelope in a concerted effort to discover its owner played through my brain like an old black-and-white horror movie. Putting a return address in the corner of the envelope seemed almost ludicrous.

My thoughts turned to the envelope's contents. I'd created a handmade anniversary card for my parents' fifty-fifth wedding anniversary. If I failed to put my signature on the card, would others be able to discern its sender? The card's design and my choice of materials spoke clearly of my personality. Then, of course, there was the nearly illegible note I'd scribbled inside. I doubt if anyone could duplicate that handwriting. The words I wrote did more than hint at my identity. I spoke of missing my parents and wishing my husband, my three boys, my daughter-in-law, and I could all spend this special day with them. Since neither of my sisters have three sons, there is no doubt my parents would know which daughter wrote the text.

How do we mark our surroundings? I'm not just talking about the documents we sign or the chocolate fingerprints our kids leave on the walls. What about evidence that isn't obvious? Do we contaminate other lives with bitterness and our sour attitudes, or do others find sweet traces of encouragement and helpfulness when we depart?

How many times have I walked away from a bad situation wrongly believing that no one could track my sin? A harsh word to an unfamiliar sales clerk, a lazy attitude when we think no one is looking, or simply a greedy little thought willfully dwelt upon—whether we think about it or not, each of these leaves a fingerprint.

Does God care? We are his children. In the same way that I want my boys to grow up to be encouraging and helpful men, I am certain our Father in heaven would rather his children leave positive tracks instead of negative ones. What sort of fingerprints are you leaving behind today?

> Create in me a clean heart, O God, and put a new and right spirit within me.
>
> Psalm 51:10

Sweet Poetry

Chocolate Poetry

O
for a
bite of
lip luscious
chocolate on my
fudgehungry tongue!
That would be lovely and flavory
and so butterwonderful
for one
such
as
I.

Ann H. Crediford

20

Good or Evil?

"Would you like skim milk, whole milk, or cream in that?" the counter clerk asked.

What would I *like*? I knew the answer, but I hesitated nonetheless. It was bad enough that I had entered this calorie-laden den of doughnut iniquity, but now I was being tempted to order their deadliest chocolate-coffee concoction weighted down with heavy cream.

It was one of the first summerlike mornings of late spring. My normal routine had been interrupted by personal errands, so here I was looking for cool relief as the sun pushed its way into the sky. Across from me was a huge photo of the shop's signature beverage. The frost on the cup shimmered as two small droplets ran slowly down its side. I could almost taste the icy, rich combination of coffee and chocolate that seemed whipped to a frenzy just for me.

The clerk patiently smiled at me while I contemplated my dilemma. There were no other customers, and she had plenty of time to seduce my taste buds. "Hey, why don't you treat yourself to the cream? You can cut back on the calories at lunch."

That was easy for her to say! On this young woman's worst day of overindulgence, she would weigh in at ninety-nine pounds. I gained more watching the doughnuts sit on the shelf than this slip of a girl would gain if she ate every single fried fritter in the place.

My resolve began to weaken. *If I choose the skim milk, I will only feel deprived and eat more later*, I told myself. *I'll just have a salad for lunch to compensate for my indulgence.*

"Make it cream," I told the patient girl.

"Good for you," she responded, grinning her victory.

When I arrived at work, a co-worker stopped me in the hall. "Hey, don't forget, we have that catered luncheon for Kate today."

The straw through which I was sipping my rich concoction nearly choked me as I struggled to respond. "Luncheon?"

"Don't tell me you forgot. They're having it catered by that Italian place down the road. I don't know the whole menu, but I do know they'll be serving chicken marsala and penne pasta with lobster sauce."

"Um . . . sure I'm coming. Wouldn't miss Kate's going-away party." I forced a bit of small talk, then exited, tossing the last of the beverage into the trash as I went.

Why did I order that calorie-glutted drink? I thought. A groan escaped as my mind ran through the exercise needed to take off those unhealthy pounds. *If only that girl hadn't talked me into the drink with heavy cream!*

Then my conscience spoke. Because both chocolate and coffee are my weakness, walking into a doughnut/coffee shop before lunch was not the smartest thing I've ever done. I talked myself into the purchase and could only hold one person accountable.

Deliberate sin is nothing to take lightly, but it is comforting to know that even those in the early church found themselves tempted. We serve a gracious God, and he is willing to forgive any action for which we confess sincere regret. There may be earthly consequences for what we do, but in God's eyes forgiveness is unquestionable.

> I do not understand my own actions. For I do not do what I want, but I do the very thing I hate. . . . For I know that nothing good dwells within me, that is, in my flesh. I can will what is right, but I cannot do it. . . . There is therefore now no condemnation for those who are in Christ Jesus. For the law of the Spirit of life in Christ Jesus has set you free from the law of sin and of death.
>
> Romans 7:15, 18; 8:1–2

Recipe to Relish

Viennese Coffee

½ cup bittersweet chocolate chips
2½ cups strong coffee
4 Tbsp. light cream
prepared whipped cream
dash of cinnamon
dash of unsweetened cocoa powder

Brew 2½ cups of very strong coffee. Melt the chocolate in a saucepan. Slowly stir in the light cream, blending well. Add the coffee and whisk the mixture until it begins to froth. Pour the mixture into cups and top each cup with whipped cream. Garnish with cinnamon and cocoa.

21

Mistaken Identity

It was that time again. Our town's volunteer fire department was hosting its annual fund-raiser. Contributions to this event take the form of beautifully beribboned and wrapped objects, tucked into pretty baskets or fancy open-sided boxes. These are auctioned off to the highest bidder. Each year I try to come up with a contribution that is a little different from the others. With my youngest heading off to college, I was feeling particularly nostalgic, and my thoughts traveled back to simpler times.

When my kids were young, money was a little tight. Instead of taking our brood to the movies or the mall, we spent evenings sprawled across our living room floor with games like Chutes and Ladders. As my boys got older, my house was often full of teens desperate to buy Boardwalk, creatively inventing words with the letters *X* and *Q*, or risking their hard-earned paper investments on the roll of the dice. It was this walk down memory lane that made me decide on a board game bonanza basket for my gift to the auction.

The writer in me could not resist word-related games. Scrabble and Boggle were two of the first I picked up. Risk, a favorite game of my young men, came shortly thereafter. Armloads of boxes later, I pulled off the shelf yet one more game that flooded my mind with wonderful memories—Candy Land.

Like many a young girl, I imagined my share of knights in shining armor and fairy forests. Unlike the average child, I often awoke from my sleep having tasted a chocolate river and taffy mushrooms. It's no wonder I loved to play Candy Land. The game's paper cards, covered with brightly colored squares, were well worn in the Bergmann household.

With only a cursory thought to what I was doing, I opened the game box right in the store. I lifted out the game board and scanned it for what I remembered as my favorite place—the dark fudge lake.

The muscles in my jaw sagged, and my knees grew weak. It wasn't there. The board looked exactly as I remembered it, only the big, sticky, fudge lake was actually a molasses swamp! Could I have been wrong all these years?

I made my purchases and ran home. After checking a few Internet sites, I came to the sad conclusion that the glorious fudge lake I had always been so eager for my sister to get stuck in was never a fudge lake at all.

Memories can be tricky things. One event can so traumatize an individual that life is thereafter defined by that event. Others somehow manage to ignore a mountain of hard times in order to build a satisfying future.

God does not ask us to turn molasses into hot fudge simply because we prefer one to the other. He wants us to see things clearly. He knows all about the evil people who lay traps in sticky swamps, but he asks us to look forward and keep an eye out for the peppermint forests he planted to lift our spirits and ease our way.

I no longer dream of lands with cotton candy clouds. My dreams are made of more solid stuff. Streets paved with transparent gold and city gates carved from a single pearl are my usual fare. Some dreams do come true.

And the twelve gates are twelve pearls, each of the gates is a single pearl, and the street of the city is pure gold, transparent as glass.

Revelation 21:21

Recipe to Relish

Easy Fudge Sauce

¾ cup sugar
⅓ cup unsweetened cocoa powder
1 Tbsp. cornstarch
¾ cup water
1 Tbsp. butter or margarine
1 tsp. vanilla extract

In a small pan, mix the first 4 ingredients. Stir over medium heat until the mixture comes to a slow boil. Remove from heat, then add the remaining ingredients. Stir until butter (or margarine) melts and the mixture is smooth. Refrigerate until ready to use. Makes 1 cup.

22

Coercion

I watched in astonishment as my young friend Melody pleaded with her daughter to eat dinner.

"Come on, honey. Take just one more bite," Melody begged.

Her daughter sat slumped in silence, her lips drawn into a scowl.

"How about some milk, Caroline? Just a few more sips and you'll have finished the glass. Remember? We're having chocolate ice cream later this afternoon. You don't have to finish your lunch, but I do want you to finish your milk," my friend continued. Her attempt at a firm tone was diminished by the fact that her words contained more compromise than insistence.

"I'll take one sip," the six-year-old offered, apparently accustomed to negotiating with her mother on such issues.

"Good girl!" Melody responded. Her face fairly beamed with pleasure.

The girl kept her eyes fixed on her mother as she placed the glass to her mouth. The milk barely touched her lips. Confident that she'd won the battle, Caroline quickly set the glass down and sent a huge smile in our direction. My friend, thrilled with what she perceived to be her daughter's compliance, tossed open arms around the little princess and gave her a quick squeeze.

I sat in stunned silence. I'd seen this woman negotiate quarter-million-dollar deals with men twice her size. How did this little slip of a child wield power over her?

As my friend and I cleared the table, we chatted. "How on earth did you get your kids to eat when they were young?" she asked.

Trying to make light of the situation I responded, "I've never had much of a problem getting my boys to eat. If it doesn't move faster than they do, they'll probably eat it."

My friend brought cups of coffee to the table, then placed her chin in her hands and looked at me with earnest eyes.

"Seriously, what did you do that made them so happy to try different foods and eat whatever you prepared? I make all of Caroline's favorite meals. She seems happy enough when I set it down in front of her, but then she hardly touches it. I've written her name on hot dogs with mustard and made grilled cheese sandwiches into clowns. Still, she only takes a bite or two, and then we fight to get her to take one or two more. Why didn't your boys fuss?"

I sensed it was time for the truth.

"Melody, when my boys were little we didn't have a lot of money, and I was not about to let anything go to waste. If one of the boys didn't want to eat, I never fought with them. I simply wrapped it in foil and put it in the fridge. If they got hungry later, I brought out what they didn't finish. I didn't have the option to give them something else. I figured if they were hungry they would eat, and if they didn't eat they weren't hungry."

"Oh, but Caroline hardly eats a thing. She'd starve if I didn't bribe and nag her."

"Really? Most things in life are not negotiable. God gives his children free will and then allows consequences to fall dependent on our choices. Caroline is not learning about those consequences. You fix it so that she can always have her chocolate ice cream when she wants it. God directs his children to things that are good for them, not necessarily to things that taste good. That helps make us strong."

Melody set her coffee cup down and folded her hands.

"I know you're right. I've been thinking along these lines for days, but I just couldn't get myself to act on it. Would you pray with me? I don't know if I can do this on my own."

"Of course we can pray. What you don't have the strength to do, God will do for you."

> You have given me the shield of your salvation, and your help has made me great. You have made me stride freely, and my feet do not slip; . . . for you girded me with strength.
>
> 2 Samuel 22:36–37, 40

Recipe to Relish

Chocolate Chocolate-Chip Ice Cream—in a Bag

Makes 1 serving

Ingredients

1 gallon-size freezer zip-seal plastic bag
1 quart-size freezer zip-seal plastic bag
½ cup whole milk
1 Tbsp. sugar
¼ tsp. vanilla
1 Tbsp. instant hot cocoa mix
2 Tbsp. mini chocolate chips

Also needed

6 Tbsp. kosher salt

ice cubes or crushed ice

Place the ingredients in the quart-size bag and zip shut. Fill the gallon-size bag halfway with ice and then sprinkle the ice with the kosher salt. Place the small bag inside the large bag and zip that one shut as well. Toss the bags around for 5 to 10 minutes or until the mixture inside the smaller bag solidifies. Remove the quart-size bag and rinse excess salt from the exterior. The ice cream can be eaten right from the small bag, or it can be scooped into a dish.

23
Cheap Chocolate

I wiped a smudge of chocolate from my chin even as I readied my fork for another mouthful of the delectable cake. "This icing is absolutely *wonderful*," I mumbled through the crumbs.

My friend grinned at my enthusiasm while she handed me a second napkin. "I told you it would be worth the trip over here."

I nodded, washing down the last bite with coffee before asking, "Can I have the recipe? John would absolutely flip for this icing."

"Sure," she said, scribbling the directions on a notepad. "But I warn you, the chocolate I used is expensive and tough to find. I had to order it a month ago."

Not two days later I stood in front of my stove, melting chocolate for my own batch of icing. We were having guests for dinner that night. I'd baked a red velvet cake that just ached to be topped with my friend's luscious icing. Not having the time or the funds to order the extravagant brand of chocolate she'd suggested, I simply substituted ordinary grocery store variety chocolate chips.

I whipped the butter, sugar, cream, and vanilla until firm peaks formed in the mixing bowl. Then I slowly added the cooled chocolate. The bowl's mountain of white fluff quickly turned to beautiful mocha clouds. I pulled out my pedestal cake dish, centered the moist cake on its crystal base, and began to mound the frosting atop the cake. With each swirl it began to look more like something from a gourmet bakery. I even laced the edges of the cake with fresh mint leaves. Its presentation would be perfect.

The meal was an irrefutable success. My table setting rivaled those of the most sophisticated homes, the food was faultlessly prepared, and the conversation could not have been more lively or enjoyable. The only thing left was to serve the dessert. I ground the freshly roasted, whole bean coffee and prepared a pot of gourmet brew. While I waited for the coffee to finish, I readied the cake plates and dessert forks.

"Oh my, that cake is beautiful!" my friend said, admiring my handiwork. "I came in here to see if you needed any help, but it's obvious you have everything well under control."

A flush came to my cheeks in response to her compliment. "Oh, you're going to love this cake recipe too. It's so good it's almost unbelievable."

"I can't wait."

We moved back into the dining room, and I served generous slices of the cake to my guests. The conversation continued pleasantly, but to my great surprise no one mentioned how wonderful the cake was. After pouring the coffee I sat down and eagerly dug a fork into my own slice. Serious disappointment surfaced. Where was that rich flavor I had experienced at my friend's house? Oh, the cake was nice enough—chocolate always is—but the taste was nothing to rave about.

It took me only a moment to figure out what happened. I used inferior ingredients—cheap chocolate—and I got out of the recipe exactly what I put in. You can't make a Tiffany tiara out of dime store rhinestones and plastic.

When we someday stand before the Creator of the universe, our deeds will be put to the test. No cheap ingredients will receive praise from him. Only those good works done in the name of Jesus will pass the test.

> Do your best to present yourself to God as one approved by him, a worker who has no need to be ashamed, rightly explaining the word of truth.
>
> 2 Timothy 2:15

Fun Fact

Chocolate syrup was used for blood in the famous forty-five-second shower scene in Alfred Hitchcock's black-and-white thriller *Psycho*. The scene actually took seven days to shoot.

24

Praying for You

There they were again, those lines oft repeated in times of trouble by well-meaning Christians across America—"I'm praying for you, dear." "You're in my prayers." "Of course I'll be praying." "I'll keep you in my prayers!"

I watched the face of the young woman receiving the comments. Her mouth was framed in a firm smile, but there was the faintest quiver to her lip and her eyes glistened with traces of moisture.

"Thank you all for your prayers. I know God will provide what I need."

I waited until the fellowship broke up and then followed the young woman to the nursery. I saw a friend of mine catch her arm a moment before she entered the door and gently steer her away from the other mothers gathering to pick up their children.

"You don't know me well, and I apologize for eavesdropping on your conversation downstairs, but I think I might be able to help you out," my friend offered.

"What do you mean?" the young woman asked.

"You mentioned that you don't have anyone to watch your daughter while you go to work. I'm home during the day with my own kids, and it would be no bother for me to watch your daughter. Our pastor will vouch for me, and I'll be happy to supply the names of some other women I've babysat for if that will make you more comfortable."

There was hesitation in her voice, but longing slipped into her words as well. "Thank you, but I can't pay you to do that. My husband left a few months ago, and I'm barely paying my other bills."

"Oh, I don't expect you to pay me," my friend answered quickly. "I'm home anyway, and having a playmate for my daughter would be great. I just want to help."

"But I work in the city and leave very, very early. I would have to drop her off at 6:00 a.m."

"Still not a problem. I'm always up that early."

Her eyes grew wide with hope, but uncertainty still edged her voice. "Why are you doing this?"

"Because I'm a Christian and you need help. It doesn't make much sense to pray for God to help you if I'm not willing to roll up my sleeves and do his work. There comes a time when God asks all of us to put our money, or our time, where our mouth is," she said.

"But I'll never be able to pay you back," she replied, tears now spilling onto her cheeks.

I watched from the corner of my misting eyes as my friend put an arm around the young woman's shoulder and said, "You just get yourself back on your feet. When you do, you'll be able to help someone else. We're all a part of the body of Christ. When you help someone else, it will be just like you're helping me."

I later found out that the young woman, a new Christian, was regularly invited to stay for dinner at my friend's home. After initially rejecting my friend's offers, the mother finally said yes, and the pleasant experience turned into a weekly ritual. After-dinner cups of coffee and slices of chocolate cake spurred leisurely conversations that greatly strengthened her faith. I wish I could say her marriage was restored and her husband came to know Christ, but that was not the case. What did happen was that a babysitting arrangement allowed her to feel her heavenly Father's strong arms, and she in turn helped many others come to know the love of her Lord.

I encourage you to put your hands as well as your prayers to work for his sake.

> And one of you says to them, "Go in peace; keep warm and eat your fill," and yet you do not supply their bodily needs, what is the good of that?
>
> James 2:16

Fun Fact

Chocolate is the number one food craved by women across North America, and it is second (pizza was first) among North American men. North Americans spend 8.9 billion dollars per year on chocolate, and each person consumes nearly twelve pounds during the course of a year.

25

Babies

My co-worker had gone to retrieve a file from the back room, and I was occupying myself as best I could until her return. Scattered on every wall and across her desk were dozens of photos. Most were of her grandchildren doing the adorable things small children do in front of a camera. When she returned I asked her about one picture in particular.

"What happened to that poor child?" I said, pointing to a picture of one very unhappy young boy.

The corners of her mouth turned up as she caressed the photo ever so slightly with the tip of her finger. "That was the first time Ryan tasted green beans."

I laughed, remembering my own children's exposure to the world of green vegetables. "I guess it's an acquired taste, like coffee. But you'd think that survival instincts would make children love green beans. I mean they're full of vitamins and all kinds of good stuff."

"That's true, but every mother knows that kids have to be hungry to eat green beans willingly—and you don't dare feed them applesauce first. They'd just as soon starve as have the green beans after they've tasted sweet fruit."

My grin grew wider as I shared my thoughts on the matter. "Adults aren't much better. It takes a lot of effort for me to stay away from candy or coffee. I'd gladly choose a mocha cappuccino over veggies. The only reason I don't is because I know I can't live on chocolate and caffeine—although there are days I might try."

We both laughed as I took the file I'd come for and headed back to my desk. When I arrived I saw the message light blinking on my phone. I found that my husband was stopping by the discount grocer on the way home. He needed to pick up fresh vegetables and salad fixings for our church dinner the next day. One of my favorite side dishes, green beans amandine à la DuMont, was planned. For this dish my husband browns bits of prosciutto or capicola in butter along with the almonds. The results are fabulous.

My husband also prepares a wonderful salad. He uses some rather bitter tasting greens, but when he tops it with his homemade raspberry-honey vinaigrette dressing—wow! The combination makes me sing praises to heaven.

Neither fare is something I would give to a newborn. Their stomachs and their taste buds would not take well to them. It requires a developed palate and a mature digestive system to appreciate and assimilate the complicated textures, tastes, and ingredients adults enjoy.

Spiritual food works the same way. Young Christians start out with God's version of mother's milk. It fills their nutritional needs, is easily digested, and tastes good. It is also dished out in small portions with extra loving care. As we grow spiritually God provides more substantial foods. Some, like pureed fruit and cereal, still taste good but require a little more digestion. Others, like green beans and squash, don't go down as easily. We try to reject those truths and beg for more fruit. But God knows what is best. We can't survive on fruit alone, so he takes the sweet away until our appetites grow strong enough to take in what we need. As our spiritual bodies grow stronger, God may send a few bitter tasting greens our way. But he never leaves our sides throughout the experience, and like the sweet raspberry-honey vinaigrette, his presence makes the experience well worth it.

The key is to eat what is right for us. An adult who still craves nothing but mother's milk is not much of an adult. Are you growing, maturing, and seeking the best that God provides for you? Or are you still throwing a temper tantrum and asking to be spoon-fed when God calls you to pick up a fork and feed on a feast of meat and potatoes?

> For though by this time you ought to be teachers, you need someone to teach you again the basic elements of the oracles of God. You need milk, not solid food; for everyone who lives on milk, being still an infant, is unskilled in the word of righteousness. But solid food is for the mature, for those whose faculties have been trained by practice to distinguish good from evil.
>
> Hebrews 5:12–14

Fun Fact

According to a survey by the American Chocolate Manufacturers Association, approximately 60 percent of all Americans give at least one gift of boxed chocolates during the winter holidays.

26

Plans and Surprises

Young boys thrive on surprise. Finding treasure in the backyard, taking unplanned neighborhood excursions, and watching a wild card team win the big game all bring pleasure to this untamed lot. Boys also love to play tricks on each other. When the tables turn and they get a dose of their own medicine, it only feeds the fire and spurs them to bigger and more elaborate schemes.

I think the unknown element in the center of an assorted chocolate is the reason young boys can't help but love these candies. I used to think it was the chewy, sweet candy they fell for, but now I know better. Boys are more interested in discovering what's in the center. It doesn't seem to matter whether they get a caramel or a jelly. Allow a boy to eat as many pieces as he pleases, and he'll gladly work his way from one side of the box to the other simply to find out what is inside every piece.

Exploring a box of assorted chocolates is a good analogy of the surprises God provides for us. We don't know what is inside that delectable coating, but the manufacturer does. That box of chocolates is planned right down to the little swirls on top of each luscious mound. Most chocolate makers code the top of every chocolate with a signature swirl that marks what the center holds. The person who hand dips the chocolate or the one who runs the dipping machine knows exactly what filling he or she is working with and will label each piece with the appropriate code.

We are surprised by the contents because we don't know the secret. There are a few chocolatiers, like Whitman, who print a key of what is in each of their confections. I like that because, I have to admit, I am not all that fond of being surprised.

God, like the chocolatier, knows everything about his creation. A manufacturer does not simply toss some ingredients into a bowl, hoping they will turn into a delightful confection. He does not make pretty chocolates and then forget which are cherry cordials and which are pecan clusters. Like the chocolatier, God plans his creations and marks their contents. He also gives us a key—the Bible. If you are allergic to nuts, you don't want to be surprised by them in the midst of your chocolate. Our loving Father helps us know which things we need to avoid. We only have to check the key.

Just as the chocolatier does not divulge every ingredient in his recipe or the secret to chocolate processing, God does not tell us everything he knows. God shares those things that are important for us to understand and allows us to have some fun discovering the rest.

> For now we see in a mirror, dimly, but then we will see face to face. Now I know only in part; then I will know fully, even as I have been fully known.
>
> 1 Corinthians 13:12

Fun Fact

How do you tell what filling is inside a sampler chocolate?

1. A square piece of chocolate typically contains caramel.
2. A bar usually signifies a crème filling.
3. A round mound with a swirl on top is almost always filled with a cherry or a crème.

Whitman's assorted sampler is the nation's top-selling boxed chocolate product.[1]

27

What If?

My kids and I used to play a game called "What If." What if the color of the sun was a deep lime green and the grass was an outlandish shade of flamingo pink? What if everyone in the world ate chocolate ice cream for breakfast but got asparagus for dessert? What if Mom never heard of coffee or chocolate and instead developed a taste for soured milk and pureed lima beans?

Most of these mind stretches took place during drives to and from sports practice or school. Those twenty-minute games often turned the world upside down! Our troubles evaporated on snow-laden tropical beaches, and our hopes soared into cotton candy clouds laced with raspberry jam. My oldest son's "what if" usually centered on sports. (What if I got a hundred goals in the hockey game, and I was the highest scorer ever?) My youngest son's "what if" was more likely to focus on home and family. (What if I grew up to be bigger than my brothers? His six-foot-four stature proves that some dreams do come true!) But none of my boys enjoyed this game more than Alan. Each "what if" was an adventure into the unexplored, and it was to be relished and rivaled only by the next game of "What If."

One bright and sunny day, a bit of reality crept into our usually lighthearted game. It occurred while Alan and I discussed a special project he was working on for his second grade GT (gifted and talented) class.

"What if I could build a car that ran on a track and was powered only by a person's mind. One where you wouldn't need to use your hands and feet to run it?" he asked.

"That would certainly be interesting," I countered, "but it would take a lot of track to go to all the places people wanted to go. Why would you want to build a car like that?"

"Well, Rodger won't be able to drive when he's a teenager," Alan said, referring to his cousin who fights a degenerative muscular disease. "I thought inventing a car where he wouldn't need to use his arms and legs would make him feel more like the other kids."

"Hmm . . ." I replied, unable to say more. An urge to bearhug him required my restraint.

Alan had the right idea. Take today's problems and try to fix them. Don't wring your hands about what might be or spend time dreaming about what might have been. Too many people lament the "what ifs" of this world. You might catch an engaged woman checking the almanac for a rain-free wedding date, a middle-aged man lamenting the loss of speculated funds, or a young couple fretting over their toddler's coming teen years.

Sometimes we spend so much time concentrating on the "what ifs" that we forget to do something about the "what ares."

Is God calling you to spend a few hours working at a soup kitchen, making phone calls to lonely friends, or wiping runny noses at a day-care center? Is he asking you to work with your youth program, volunteer at your public library, or teach an adult to read? Are you spending more hours watching sitcoms and dreaming about the "what ifs" than you are building relationships that will open doors for eternity? Ask God to show you "what ares" and how you can serve him today.

> As we have therefore opportunity, let us do good unto all men, especially unto them who are of the household of faith.
>
> Galatians 6:10 KJV

Fun Fact

Seventy-one percent of American chocolate eaters prefer milk chocolate.

28

Distractions

The ponds on either side of our neighborhood glistened their frozen welcome. The temperature held at the freezing mark, and my oldest son could hardly wait to get his skates on.

"Wait up, JC. I'm going with you to check the ice first," I said, grabbing my son's elbow before he lunged out the door.

"Oh, Mom. The other guys are already on the ice!"

"That may be, but I'm still going to make sure it's solid before *you* get out there."

JC impatiently shifted his weight from foot to foot while I helped his brother wiggle into a pair of boots and bundled my youngest in a snowsuit.

"You ready?" my eight-year-old asked, his hand already opening the door.

I slipped on my coat. "Yup. Let's go!" I replied.

With my one-year-old planted on my hip, I watched my five-year-old, Alan, merrily detour through every snow mound along the way. JC ran ahead, and I heard him call out to his friends, but it was not until I turned the corner that I caught sight of my oldest standing at the edge of the pond, obediently waiting for me. As soon as he saw me, he ran to the fallen log the kids used as a bench and began putting on his skates.

I sat his brothers down next to him and instructed them to mind their brother. Then I shuffled my boots onto the ice, inspecting it as I went. I moved along the sides, across the middle, and then toward the overflow. There the water still ran steadily and only a thin layer of ice covered the surface. Although the rest of the pond sported a respectable three-inch cover of ice, this area would not freeze. I turned toward the pickup hockey game at the other side of the pond and waved my oldest to join his friends—but not without a shouted reminder.

"JC, remember to stay away from the overflow. It isn't frozen."

"I know, Mom," he called as he shot past me, hockey stick already positioned for the puck.

I picked up my youngest and watched my middle son swing a stick at some ice chips, imitating his older brother. Just then I saw a wild shot fly from the far side of the pond. The puck flew across the ice, my son and two others in hot pursuit. As it hit bumps on the surface, the puck danced and spun but never slowed. The boys, too busy trying to outfinesse each other, did not seem to notice they were headed for thin ice.

"Stay here," I ordered, thrusting my youngest into his brother's arms.

Screaming a warning, I dashed across the ice, placing my frantically waving arms and spread-eagled body between the overflow and the unbridled skaters. The puck flew past me. Seconds later, amid a spray of ice chips, the three boys came to a halt only inches from me. From behind me came a crack and a splash as the puck landed in the icy water.

"Aw, we lost the puck!" one of the boys lamented.

"You can be glad that's all you lost," I fumed. "A few more feet and you'd be kicking pond scum with those blades. Pay attention to where you're going!"

The boys returned to their game somewhat subdued and minus one puck. I returned home to make hot chocolate for my younger boys and to make phone calls to the neighborhood parents. We began a series of "ice watches" that day, taking turns checking on the boys and the safety of the pond.

Sipping my hot chocolate, I had some time to reflect on the incident. The kids forgot about the dangerous overflow because they trusted in the safety of the ice already under their feet. Chasing our obsessions distracts us from life's hazards. The same happens in our Christian walk. The good times deliver security, the world diverts our attention, and calamity is ready to follow. God, like a good parent, sends reminders and shouts warnings. If we don't heed them, he may be forced to throw himself in our path. We can either stop or force our way past him. Sometimes that means we fall through the ice.

> For we ourselves were once foolish, disobedient, led astray, slaves to various passions and pleasures.
>
> Titus 3:3

Fun Fact

The first chocolate box was produced by Richard Cadbury in 1868. He decorated the cover with a picture of his daughter holding her kitten.

29

Promises, Promises

I glared at the inadequate fare presented on the reception tables. Dozens of families had promised to bring refreshments. The response to our phone calls had been very positive. Some willing parents had offered to bring more than one home-baked item, while others wanted to donate their time. As I looked over the six tables of scant contributions, I felt personally affronted that so many would offer but so few would keep their promise.

A voice came from behind me, "Oh my! Where are all the refreshments?"

I turned just as the mother of one of my son's classmates slipped into the room. I was relieved at the thought of her assistance.

"I'm glad you're here. I've been waiting for your double batch of brownies. I don't know what happened. So many people said they would bring baked goods, but it seems that not everyone followed through." I quickly turned away and returned to the task of laying out napkins, hoping she wouldn't spy the frustration I knew etched my face.

"Oh, Louise, I'm sorry! Things were so hectic with graduation coming up this week, that I only had time to bake one pan."

"Oh!" I said, the pitch of my voice rising in panic. I looked over the few baked goods spread across the refreshment tables. The bright red tablecloths beautifully complemented the miniature white carnations enrobed with halos of silver stars. I'd used the school colors, silver and red, for the disposable tableware as well. The decorations were perfect. Only one thing was lacking. We expected close to a hundred and fifty parents, students, and administrators, but we had baked goods that would barely serve half that number.

My friend glanced at her watch. "What time is this scheduled to start?"

"Eight," I responded glumly.

"Look, you finish setting up and get the coffee started. I'll be back before you know it."

"Where are you going? It's too late to get homemade cakes now!" I asked.

"Who says they have to be homemade? And who says we have to have cake? Don't worry. You make certain that everything is ready, and I'll make sure you have something to serve."

Within twenty minutes the woman was back with her arms full of goodies. As we unloaded the bags I realized she'd gone to the local grocery store and purchased prepared vegetable trays and sour cream dips. She'd also bought commercial angel food cakes, two flats of large, stemmed strawberries and a dozen jars of hot fudge, and had stopped by her house to pick up two old fondue pots. Together we set out the vegetable trays, heated the fudge, arranged the strawberries on faux silver trays, and cut the angel food cake into dipping-size squares.

It seems that fondue is quite the novelty for my children's generation and a pleasant nostalgic stroll for mine. I received numerous compliments on my choice of refreshments, which I redirected to my ingenious friend.

After the party I was still tempted to lay a few sharp remarks in the laps of those who had failed me, but God held my tongue. We are all human, and I know I've inadvertently broken some promises in my time, but their broken promises hurt nonetheless. What seemed like a small thing to them was a great inconvenience and expense for my helpful friend and me.

It's nice to know there is one who is always faithful. God cannot deny his own character by lying, and he will not change his mind or forget his promises. He is the one I can always trust.

> And he who is the Glory of Israel will not lie, nor will he change his mind, for he is not human that he should change his mind!
>
> 1 Samuel 15:29 NLT

Recipe to Relish

Chocolate-Dipped Apricots and Strawberries

high-quality bittersweet chocolate (broken into small chunks)
1 Tbsp. vegetable shortening
large dried apricots
whole shelled almonds
large fresh strawberries with stems

Melt the chocolate with shortening in the microwave or in a double boiler; let cool slightly. Take a dried apricot and find the little hole in the end where the pit was removed. Stuff an almond into the hole and dip that end into the melted chocolate, coating the apricot about halfway up. Lay the apricot on a waxed-paper-lined cookie sheet to dry. Hold a strawberry by the stem and dip three quarters of the berry into the chocolate. Lay the strawberry on a waxed-paper-lined cookie sheet to dry. Repeat this process until you get bored, get tired, or run out of one of the ingredients.

30

Red Hot

"Strike while the iron is hot!"

The phrase slid into my brain and took root like a watered seed in fertile soil. I don't remember the rest of the speaker's address. I don't even remember the topic of discussion or the point he was trying to make when he used that expression. All I remember is the thought that grew from it.

This phrase comes from a time when weapons and farm implements were formed by heating metal rods until their glowing form indicated they were pliable. The red hot metal was hammered, cooled, reheated, and hammered again. The only way to shape the iron to your will was to strike at the moment when the rod was hot and ready.

The beautiful chocolates you contemplate behind glistening display cases can only be molded into their unique forms while they are liquid. The chocolatier watches the fluid carefully—an excess of heat and the chocolate will burn, not enough heat and the chocolate will not mold.

God allows the fire in our lives to soften our stubborn spirits and mold our stiff wills. We may feel as if the change destroys who we are, but it is, instead, turning us into what we were meant to be. We remain ourselves, just as the iron remains iron, and the chocolate remains chocolate. Our usefulness, however, becomes apparent in the change.

When I was a child there was a candy called Bonomo's Turkish Taffy. I loved every flavor they made, but the banana and chocolate bars held a special place in my heart. Technically, these candies were neither taffy nor Turkish, and their flavors held little resemblance to actual chocolate or bananas—but they were delicious. If you kept a bar cold and smacked it on a table, it would break into dozens of small snack-size pieces. If you left the candy in the sun, it would soften and you could pull and stretch it out into long, gummy strings. People can be like that. Little change takes place in a cold, hard heart. It needs to be heated up a bit before it becomes pliable.

For this reason, I pray that God continues to heat up my life. I know that it may be uncomfortable, but the fine product it produces is worth the momentary distress.

> But by your hard and impenitent heart you are storing up wrath for yourself on the day of wrath, when God's righteous judgment will be revealed.
>
> Romans 2:5

Fun Facts

Do you remember what products these jingles represent?

1. B-O . . . N-O . . . M-O . . . Oh, Oh, Oh . . . it's Bonomo's . . . Caaaaaaaaaaaandy!

2. The taste of real Hershey's cocoa can easily make your whole wide world more chocolaty.
3. I'm a pepper, he's a pepper, she's a pepper, we are peppers. Wouldn't you like to be a pepper too?
4. Sometimes you feel like a nut; sometimes you don't.
5. N-E-S-T-L-E-S, Nestlé makes the very best . . . choccccccccolate.
6. Picky people pick _____ peanut butter. It's the peanut butter picky people pick.
7. You got chocolate in my peanut butter!
8. R-r-ruffles have ridges.

Answers: 1. Bonomo's Turkish Taffy, 2. Cocoa Krispies, 3. Dr Pepper, 4. Mounds and Almond Joy, 5. Nestlé Quick chocolate drink mix, 6. Peter Pan peanut butter, 7. Reese's peanut butter cups, 8. Ruffles potato chips

31

Birthday Party

My co-worker's eyes fairly danced as she told me about the surprise sixtieth birthday party she was planning for her husband. Instead of following a recent morbid trend that involved sending black invitations with "Over the Hill" and tombstones emblazoned on the front, she'd taken a much lighter, and I think more tasteful, approach to this senior milestone. Using bright yellow and red cardstock, she had made invitations with her husband's childhood photo smartly displayed on the front.

One day over lunch we talked about her party preparations. The enthusiasm she offered was delightful, but there seemed to be one thing bothering her.

"Maybe it's silly, but I made up party bags for each guest." My friend's gaze remained fastened on her food while her fork pushed the salad around her plate.

"Why would that be silly?" I asked.

"It seems a little childish," she replied.

"Nonsense. I think it's cute."

Encouraged, she smiled and continued the conversation. "I thought so too. I bought things that would remind our friends of my husband."

"Like what?"

"I put in a personalized pencil that says 'Happy 60th Birthday, Jim'—to mark this particular year. There's a racecar pencil sharpener because he loves cars, especially hot rods. I don't know if I ever told you this, but he's rebuilt some great cars over the years."

I nodded.

"I found small note pads, which I thought would be cute as a reminder that we're all getting older and our memories aren't what they used to be."

We both chuckled.

"There are a few more things—a deck of playing cards to represent his once-a-month poker games, a baseball-mitt key chain in memory of his twenty-five years playing softball and coaching the kids' leagues, and his favorite candy, Tootsie Rolls."

I laughed. "You can't beat a goody bag with a chocolate treat! You wait and see; everyone is going to love what you've done."

When I returned to my desk, I couldn't stop thinking about the party bags. It was obvious that my friend had put a great deal of thought into the items she bought. I closed my eyes and imagined her guests eating a sweet slice of chocolate birthday cake as they sipped their coffee, laughed, joked, and reminisced. One would tell a story about the night Jim's little league team made the playoffs, while another would ask about the red Corvette he had rebuilt. Each trinket would be a significant reminder of some time past and an indication that there are still many good times to come.

The Bible uses the word *remember* 142 times (NRSV). It seems to be an important word. But what does God want us to recall, and why does he want us to remember things long past? I believe he wants us to remember who sustained us in days gone by so we are mindful of who provides for us today. I think he wants us to remember the miracles of the past so we can more easily trust him with our future.

By knowing what he did, we have hope and are assured that he will provide for our future.

> I will call to mind the deeds of the LORD; I will remember your wonders of old.
>
> Psalm 77:11

Pleasant Pastime

Chocolate Party Ideas

- Hide chocolate coins around the room and have guests discover the secret treasure tucked under a magazine, atop the coffee table, and inside grandpa's slippers.

- Purchase flat chocolate bars that have slide-off exterior wrappers. On your computer create personalized candy wrappers for your event. Cut each sheet to the appropriate size and tape the wrapper securely around the candy bar. You now have perfect, customized chocolate favors for your party.

- Instead of serving sliced cake with a scoop of ice cream at your next birthday party, why not serve chocolate pizza? Start with two large disposable pizza pans. Soften one quart of chocolate ice cream. Spread the ice cream onto the pans. Top with every sort of chopped candy bar and chocolate sprinkle you can find. Freeze until firm. Serve.

- No holiday in sight? Come up with your own reason for a party. Give a "Just Because" party, a "Third Saturday in January" party, or an "I Love Chocolate" party.

32

Chocolate and Cheese

"Can I have a piece of cheese in my hand?" my oldest asked. His wild blond hair stuck up at odd angles, and I rumpled his head as I responded.

"Sure," I said, handing him a slice of yellow American cheese before returning to the lunch preparation.

I heard a "thank you" echo down the hall as he ran off. Not a minute later he was back.

"May I have another slice of cheese in my hand?"

"Not now, JC. Lunch is almost ready."

"Can I have a piece of cheese in my hand *with* my lunch?"

"I'm making cheese sandwiches. You don't need another piece of cheese."

"But you said cheese is good for my teeth. Don't you want me to have good teeth?" he asked, his smile exposing a bit of tongue through a large gap where his permanent teeth were awaiting their turn.

"Yes, but I think you've had enough cheese for right now."

"Can I have a piece of cheese for dessert?"

"I was going to let you have a brownie for dessert," I replied, smiling.

My son's brow furrowed, his face reflecting the dilemma. Then the crisis passed, and his smile returned.

"Can I have my brownie wrapped in pieces of cheese?"

We laugh at my young man's creative and persistent attempt to get the best of both worlds. Now, as a man with a family of his own, my son's creativity and persistence serve him well. Back then a brownie hemmed in by a slice of American cheese did not amuse me. Chocolate brownies are a favorite in my family. So is cheese. But wrapping one in the other didn't seem tasty.

What we wrap our personalities in is important too. Our inner spirit may contain the sweetness of Jesus, but if we cover it with something not compatible with its sweetness (arrogance, resentment, or hostility), we will not attract many people to the extraordinary gift within us.

> Above all, clothe yourselves with love, which binds everything together in perfect harmony.
>
> Colossians 3:14

Recipe to Relish

Ricotta Cake

recipe donated by Betty Dominico

1 yellow, marble, or chocolate cake mix
2 lbs. ricotta
4 eggs
1 cup sugar

1 tsp. vanilla
½ cup mini chocolate chips (optional)
1 dozen foil cupcake liners (for serving, not baking)

Prepare the cake mix as directed and pour into a greased 9 x 13 pan. In a separate bowl, mix the other ingredients until blended. Pour the ricotta mixture evenly over the cake batter. Bake at 350 degrees for 1 hour (or until center is set). Cool completely, then dust with powdered sugar. Refrigerate. When you are ready to serve the cake, cut it into small squares and place each piece in a foil cupcake liner. Present on a pretty serving platter.

33

Creative Inclinations

All three of my children displayed creative tendencies at an early age. Two of my boys, Alan and Tim, showed remarkable musical talent. Since I cannot play even a kazoo, I give credit for those musical genes to my husband. My oldest son, JC, has extraordinary problem-solving skills, displays genuine leadership, and wields a sharp wit that can be downright dangerous when he gets on a roll. My boys' ingenuity can at times boggle the mind.

I am one of those people who appreciates ingenuity translated to workable solutions. A friend recently shared her mother's solution to a dress-up dilemma. When Jeannette was a child, she and her friends wanted to be hobos for a costume party. A problem arose when they tried to create a five o'clock shadow on their sensitive, girlish faces. Not in the least taken aback, Jeannette's mother did what any sensible woman would. She turned to coffee. Apparently, a little Vaseline mixed with finely ground coffee beans turns a young lady into an unshaven hobo in no time at all!

I have another multitalented friend who consistently trims her holiday table in the most creative fashion. With a crop of young grandchildren sporting exploring fingers, she decided to put aside the fancy crystal place-card holders and instead made child-friendly, edible Christmas favors. Using little more than sugar cones, chocolate chips, and some store-bought icing, she fashioned dozens of delightful miniature Christmas trees. Not everyone appreciates creativity though. School children who make up excuses for not doing their homework are sure to fail, and the man who uses creative accounting to fix his financial records will find that the IRS is not amused.

My God is a creative God, and under the appropriate circumstances he appreciates when we activate this gift in ourselves. He loves it when I use my vivid imagination to find positive solutions to disparaging situations, and I think he smiles when I draw on my abilities to better appreciate his wondrous creation. But there are times when God tells us not to get creative and not to veer from his prescribed path. When it comes to sin, God tells us to simply stay within the boundaries he carefully sets for our safety. He asks us to use our creative talents to lift, encourage, and give grace to those who come across our paths. We are not to amuse ourselves at the expense of others.

As a writer, my imagination sometimes runs wild with stories that border on the fantastic. I may "let myself go" and write an eccentric yarn to stretch my writing ability. I may even pen such a tale simply because I find it amusing. But sooner or later I am obliged to focus my attention on the needs of the reader, not on myself. Will a lighthearted anecdote lighten someone's burden? Will a gripping suspense novel give him or her pause to reflect? Will a well-crafted romance spark a young girl's righteous or unholy desires? I've noticed two things about creativity. First, it works like a magnifying glass. Whatever is under its domain is intensified. Second, my resourceful God seems to have developed a system that blesses me when I use my creativity to lift another. No matter how much I try, I can't seem to outgive the Giver! Whether you are solving your daughter's five o'clock shadow problem with ground coffee or making ice cream cone Christmas trees to amuse your grandchildren, God will bless creativity used to enrich others.

> Each one, as a good manager of God's different gifts, must use for the good of others the special gift he has received from God.
>
> 1 Peter 4:10 GNT

Pleasant Pastime

Cone Christmas Trees

1 dozen sugar cones (the kind with a pointed tip)
1 bag semisweet chocolate chips
"stiff" canned or homemade vanilla icing
green food coloring
assorted small red and green candies

Tint icing using green food coloring. Place cones open side down on waxed paper and coat one cone with tinted icing. Gently cover surface with chocolate chips (flat side against the icing). Intersperse with occasional red and green candies for decoration. Repeat with additional cones.

Note: Do not coat all the cones at one time or the icing will form a crust and the chocolate chips will not stick.

Use as holiday table favors.

34

Wrong Line

I held the organza-draped cellophane bag higher to protect it from the crowd pressing me from behind. In front of me was a table displaying an array of beautiful Belgian confections.

"This is where they're setting up the free Belgian chocolate samples," the woman next to me whispered conspiratorially. She and I had been admiring the various chocolate offerings and sharing our obsession for the product. "I've been standing here for the good part of an hour so I would be first in line." She displayed a satisfied smile. Her arms lay across her chest in a gesture that almost begged someone to defy her.

"Are you sure this is where they're holding the tasting?" I asked. "The flier simply says it will be held at 1:00, but it doesn't say where. What if the line starts in another part of the store?"

She brushed aside my skepticism, "Just look at this table. It's the only table in the store that doesn't have a large display, and the only items scattered on it happen to be Belgian chocolates. Where else would they hand out the free samples?" Her logic seemed infallible, and a part of me was tempted to root myself to that spot just in case she was right.

Just then I heard the manager of the store announce that anyone not currently making a purchase should exit the facility.

"Those of you interested in participating in the chocolate tasting will need to join the line just outside the door, in the corridor," the manager said with a smile.

I glanced out the store window and saw my dear husband patiently holding a place for me right near the front of a long column of people. It was a good thing he paid attention to what was happening around him. I was in such a hurry to get into the store and see the merchandise and became so engrossed in my conversation with the woman that I failed to notice the sign. It instructed people where to wait for the tasting event. The woman was no more knowledgeable than I was, but in my haste to appease my appetite, I was ready to be persuaded by her words. If she had been right, it would have put me in the front of the line.

As I left the store, I could hear her venom as she argued with the manager about her right to be first in line. "I waited for nearly an hour," she said. "I should be first no matter where the line forms."

The compassionate manager reluctantly but firmly explained that she'd been waiting in the wrong place and that the tasting would not take place until the store was first cleared of all its current patrons. He suggested that she hurry to get the next place in line, but she continued to argue that she should not have to wait in the other line and that her hour of waiting at the table within the store was sufficient.

At last glance, I saw the store manager prevail. She furiously stomped toward the rear of the line, which now wound a great length around the corner and down another hallway. I had little doubt that by the time the end of the long line reached the store entrance there would be no free samples left.

So often people suppose that what they've done earns them the right to special recognition. People mistakenly believe that living good lives or doing good deeds earns them a place in heaven. Unfortunately, neither is true. At the last judgment, Jesus will sadly inform many that they've been waiting in the wrong line.

> But many who are first will be last, and the last will be first.
>
> **Mark 10:31**

Fun Fact

For the average person, a carob bar is, in fact, no more healthful than a chocolate bar. If comparable in size, they contain approximately the same amount of fat and calories.

35

Dreidels and Kings

The gold-covered chocolate coins sparkled in the evening candlelight as my children laughed and played the dreidel game with their friends. I was delighted when my children and I were invited to share in my friend's family's Hanukkah celebration. They were a Jewish family who knew and loved their Messiah, Jesus, but continued to enjoy the traditional celebrations connected with their heritage. Although they celebrated the birth of Christ at Christmas, my friend was careful to teach her children the many traditions associated with Jewish feasts and festivals.

I was recently reminded of that evening and of those chocolate coins when I attended a seminar on Aztec history. In this society cacao (chocolate) beans were used as money. One of the Aztecs' ancient texts listed the annual tribute paid to their ruler. Along with countless exotic animal skins and valuable pots of grain, one town was required to pay approximately 4,840,000 cacao beans. That's a whole lot of chocolate, considering that chocolate beans, like most food products, spoil if they aren't processed or preserved. Did the Aztec king have a hearty appetite for hot cocoa?

As it happens, he did have a fervent taste for the bean, but before he consumed the tribute, he needed to dole out a portion of the beans to compensate his workers for their service or for products they provided. Since the Aztec people could not store this wealth, the populace quickly turned their salaries into purchased goods. Eventually, those shopkeepers would pay their taxes with the cacao beans, and the beans would find their way back to the emperor, who would have the cacao ground to a fine powder for his ceremonial drinks. Because individuals were unable to accumulate great wealth, the economics of Aztec society were kept on a nice, even keel. Life was not perfect, but the Aztec people were reasonably equal financially.

Today churches habitually procrastinate when it comes to talking about money, but Jesus did not shy away from this issue. Once, a man of some position asked how he could get to heaven. Christ told him to keep the law, and the young man proudly replied that he kept all the scriptural laws. Then Jesus gently told him that there was one more thing he needed to do. The young ruler was to give away his riches and accept the simple life of a disciple. The Bible says that the man left very sad. Some think money was the issue, but it was not—love was. This man loved the temporary comfort money could provide more than he loved Jesus. The sparkle of the gold coins and the delicious taste of chocolate do not in the slightest compare with the gift of God's precious presence.

Keep your lives free from the love of money, and be content with what you have; for he has said, "I will never leave you or forsake you."

Hebrews 13:5

For where your treasure is, there your heart will be also.

Luke 12:34

Fun Fact

Some people are concerned about the caffeine in chocolate. The truth is that an ounce of milk chocolate has about six milligrams of caffeine. That is about the same amount as one cup of decaffeinated coffee. One cup of drip brewed coffee contains at least a hundred milligrams of caffeine.

36

Café Chocolat

As I clutched my iced coffee and peered into the display case at Café Chocolat, I swallowed hard. Before me were dozens and dozens of the most decadent chocolate confections imaginable. Enticingly strange were confections of chocolate mousse formed into pyramidlike shapes and served on clouds of whipped cream. More standard fare included éclairs with shiny chocolate crowns and milk-chocolate-mousse-filled cream puffs dusted with cocoa powder. Each stood in their rows like little soldiers awaiting orders. Miniature raspberry tarts with white chocolate crusts and cakes that boasted names like "blackout blizzard" and "chocolate-peanut heaven" bore their share of the acclaim.

What finally held my attention, though, were the tiny individual cakes. One held a small placard with the name "white carnation." The dense, flourless chocolate cake was covered in bittersweet chocolate with a large white chocolate carnation festooning its cap. It looked simple enough, but I knew that breaking into this confection would reveal the wondrous complexity of its creation.

After I pointed out the desire of my heart, the clerk retrieved it with just a hint of reluctance and a measure of envy etched into his features. His eyes told me what I already knew—this was the dessert of a lifetime. I sat at my little café stool, awaiting the arrival of my sweet like a queen awaiting her coronation crown.

That morsel satisfied the depth of my culinary soul more than any sweet before or since. I took great pleasure in each forkful and managed to savor even those crumbs that strove to elude my capture.

Oh, God, that I would wait with the same eagerness and relish with equal passion each portion of your Word served to me.

> Your words were found, and I ate them, and your words became to me a joy and the delight of my heart; for I am called by your name, O Lᴏʀᴅ, God of hosts.
>
> Jeremiah 15:16

Recipe to Relish

Flourless Chocolate Truffle Cake

16 oz. semisweet chocolate chips
1¼ sticks (10 Tbsp./5 oz.) unsalted butter
5 eggs, separated and at room temperature
chocolate curls (optional)

Note: The key to this cake is room temperature eggs.

Preheat oven to 375 degrees. Generously butter (unsalted butter is preferred) a 9-inch round springform pan.

Melt chocolate chips and 1¼ sticks butter in double boiler (or in microwave). Stir until smooth. Cool.

Pour chocolate into a large bowl. Beat yolks in a small mixing bowl, then pour the yolks into the chocolate and blend well. Beat egg whites to stiff peaks in a separate bowl. Fold a small amount of the whites into the chocolate-yolk mixture to loosen the chocolate. Then fold in the remaining whites. Pour batter into the prepared pan and bake 12 minutes. DO NOT OVERBAKE. Cake will be loose and will firm up when refrigerated.

Cool completely in the pan. Refrigerate overnight before removing the sides of the springform pan. Decorate with chocolate curls if desired. Makes 14 to 16 thin wedges.

37

Trash to Treasure

The sign beckoned me from the street. It read, "From Trash to Treasure." The small shop intrigued me, but my mind took a strange turn when I contemplated the name. Visions of banana peels and rusted tin artwork danced in my head. Did I want to venture through the door? I steeled myself against the ridiculous images in my brain and turned my car into the parking lot.

As I entered, my senses were assailed with the delectable scents of coffee and chocolate. This made the treasure most evident, but the gay colors, the fresh flowers, and the store's impeccable cleanliness gave no evidence of trash. Upon further inspection, however, I found clues to that portion of the name.

The ingenious owner had taken discarded furniture and turned the pieces into beautiful, functional objects of art. Painted in every imaginable hue, child-size dressers danced with circus animals and balloons, vanities exhibited spring floral sprays, and kitchen cupboards flaunted hand-painted herbal displays of every kind. Now, as intriguing as these were, what really caught my attention were the smaller offerings.

Discarded fruit and vegetable crates were cleaned, sanded, and painted in an array of crayon colors. Old pots, tins, boxes, and canvas bags were refurbished and now housed the most delectable treats. Homemade chocolates, cocoa mixes, bags of gourmet coffee, brownie and coffee-cake mixes, and chocolate-coated spoons were packed together with colorful mugs and other beautiful crockery and cutlery.

My amazement grew with each gift item. No two were the same. This creative owner fashioned a unique arrangement for each piece of merchandise. An old washboard was cleaned, painted, and transformed into a kitchen message board. She packed it with small parcels of flavored coffee and hand-stamped recipe cards. A huge old laundry spoon was painted a brilliant cyan blue. Brass hooks were inserted along the handle, and when hung horizontally, the spoon would hold keys, mittens, and other small items usually left by the front door.

Thoughts of items stored in my basement made me cringe. I could never hope to turn them into useful gifts, but perhaps the owner of this shop would consider my trash a sweet donation to her cause. Maybe she would see beyond the broken dishes and cracked coat rack. Maybe it wasn't trash at all, but simply undiscovered treasure!

That was when a less pleasant thought slipped quietly to the front of my brain. How long have I accumulated rubbish in my heart and mind? What if my trash were turned over to the ultimate creative being of the universe? Would God bring treasure out of my mess? Are my broken dreams and cracked attempts at love simply treasures waiting to be discovered?

God spoke to my heart in that moment of clarity. Good does not come out of evil, but a broken good thing is not evil. It is simply temporarily out of use. Out of a good heart, a heart that loves God, the Creator can and will produce treasures. What broken treasures can you offer him today?

> The good person out of the good treasure of the heart produces good, and the evil person out of the evil treasure produces evil; for it is out of the abundance of the heart that the mouth speaks.
>
> Luke 6:45

Recipe to Relish

Monkey Pops

2 bananas
3 Tbsp. instant hot cocoa mix
1½ Tbsp. milk
2 Tbsp. honey
½ tsp. vanilla extract
4 Popsicle sticks
coconut, chopped peanuts, sprinkles (optional)

Mix the cocoa, milk, vanilla, and honey. Peel the bananas. Cut each banana in half to make 4 pieces. Roll the banana halves in the chocolate mixture. Make sure each is well coated. Then roll the bananas in one of the optional items (if desired). Place 1 popsicle stick into the cut end of the banana. Place on a waxed-paper-coated cookie sheet and freeze until firm. Serve. Makes 4 pops.

38

Shimmer and Shine

I studied the objects before me with utter fascination. Great care had been taken with each detail. The glossy finish of the chocolate, the moist appearance of the cake crumbs, and the airiness of the whipped topping all made my mouth water. It was nearly impossible to believe these items were made of glass.

A friend had directed me to an unusual curio shop in a nearby town. While inspecting their wares I'd come across a display of glass items made to look like edible treats. There were boxes shaped like giant hero sandwiches. Lift off the top slice of bread, and you would find a neat container for trinkets. I saw pies whose upper crusts concealed functional pie plates. Dangling from nearly invisible threads was an assortment of what appeared to be glittering wrapped hard candies, ready to be hung from a Christmas tree but never to be tasted. My favorites were the paperweights. They included a slice of chocolate cake slathered with mocha icing, a small dish of strawberry ice cream festooned with fresh strawberry slices, and an askew stack of chocolate sandwich cookies nearly ready to topple.

I almost bought the cookie paperweight but at the last moment decided against it. The glass art was beautiful, but it lacked something. The warmth and the smell of a homemade apple pie were not in the pie plate. The artist had nearly captured the texture of the strawberries and creaminess of the ice cream, but the chill and the scent were missing. And, of course, one would never taste the rich chocolate flavor that should accompany a slice of devil's food cake. These were all amusing replicas but could not rival the genuine articles. The thought of staring at a stack of inedible chocolate sandwich cookies sitting on my desk was a bit unsettling.

I'm afraid there are Christians who come across a lot like these objets d'art. Like the wrapped candy ornaments, they might be mistaken for the real thing by a casual observer. But upon closer examination an individual would soon discover the true nature of the object.

Although there is nothing wrong with glass art objects made to look like sweet treats, I want those who scrutinize my life to not only see the image of Christ but smell and taste the essence of Jesus in me. I want my fragrant aroma to attract those who are tempted to simply pass by. I want the taste of what I offer to satisfy the hunger of those who talk and walk with me. I want to be a genuine Christian, not some pretty imitation.

> So that the genuineness of your faith . . . may be found to result in praise and glory and honor when Jesus Christ is revealed.
>
> 1 Peter 1:7

Fun Facts

Chocolate-Loving Louis

In the seventeenth century, chocolate was a scarce and costly commodity. Only the most comfortable segments of society could afford such luxury. When the Spanish princess Maria Theresa was betrothed to Louis XIV of France, she chose a very special gift for her groom-to-be. She sent him a present of chocolate in an ornate chest.

Late in the 1600s, a Frenchman by the name of David Chaillon discovered how to remove most of the liquid from chocolate. This allowed the product to be molded and made it both more portable and, when combined with sugar, more palatable. Louis XIV was so pleased that he appointed Chaillon to the newly created position of royal chocolate maker to the king. In this position he enjoyed a twenty-three-year monopoly on French chocolate sales.

39

Seizing the Moment

"That's it!" my friend shouted into the phone. "I've had it with those people. All I've ever done is try to make peace. I give and give, and then I'm expected to give some more. Well, I'm done with them. You hear me? No more! I'm done forgiving them."

I let my friend rant as I silently prayed on the other end of the phone. We'd been down this road before. She was a person who usually put forth a maximum effort, but she was also someone who let pent-up emotions take her to the brink of disaster. Minor problems could bring down her positive expectations like a breeze topples a cleverly stacked house of cards. I wasn't sure that compromise was possible in her current situation, but I had a feeling that none was even being sought. When I finally hung up the phone, it was with a frustrated *click*. While washing my hands in preparation for my next task, I couldn't shake the lingering feeling that I should have done more to help.

Turning to my stove, I began preparing a chocolate coating that would decorate my next batch of Christmas cookies. My mind remained occupied with thoughts of my friend, but I was determined to move forward with my chores nonetheless. As the chocolate melted in my double boiler, I failed to notice a small drop of water that ran from my hand, down the spoon, and into the pot. If I had been paying closer attention, I might have seen the bead set off on its path, but as it was I didn't notice the droplet until it had reached the glistening coating. The chocolate's reaction to its intruder was instantaneous. The mixture seized and immediately became a thick, uncooperative blob.

I shut off the stove with a sigh and set my spoon down on the counter. One single drop of water had ruined the whole pot of coating. I stared at the useless glob that sat before me. I had only two choices. I could chuck the mess and start over with a clean, dry pot and fresh chocolate, or I could attempt to fix the seized mixture by slowly reheating it after working in a bit of vegetable oil. Not having any more coating chips, I decided to see if I could redeem the wreckage.

Some praying, some stirring, and some time later, I was rewarded with a lovely pot of glossy melted chocolate, and the original batch was not wasted.

Later that afternoon I nibbled one of the sweet, chocolate-coated cookies while enjoying a hot cup of coffee. My fixer-upper cookies were delicious. Not only were my ingredients redeemed but also a biblical truth set itself in my spirit even as the chocolate on the cookies set.

Individuals in our society are quick to toss out anything we don't find serviceable. Worn clothes are no longer mended. When they are torn or out of style, we replace them with something new. If a marriage doesn't suit us, we trash it and get a new one.

Jesus is not like that. He is the ultimate fixer of damaged goods. Ever patient, he stands quietly stirring our pot, gently coaxing us with a little more oil until we glisten with sweet delight. He doesn't give up on us. Alleluia!

> Be imitators of me, as I am of Christ.
>
> 1 Corinthians 11:1

Fun Fact

According to the Chocolate Manufacturers Association, in the year 2000 there were approximately 300,000 paid employees in chocolate and confectionery industries.

40

Diamonds

I sipped my coffee slowly with a small plate of chocolate-draped petits fours balanced carefully on my knee.

"Her smile sure says it all, doesn't it?" the woman sitting next to me asked.

I nodded in agreement. "Those two were meant for each other. I'm so happy they got engaged. And did you see that ring? It's absolutely beautiful!"

"It isn't a large diamond, but it sure is perfect. The setting really suits the cut of the stone, and that diamond sparkles like nothing I've ever seen before," she continued.

"It must be a perfect, or near perfect, diamond," I admitted.

A smile spread across her face. "A perfect diamond for the perfect couple. Can't beat that."

Looking at the diminutive cakes on my plate, I began imagining the pastry chef who had prepared them. His eyes squinted as he positioned his pastry bag over each shiny, chocolate-covered morsel. With great attention to detail, he held his breath as he applied the first petal, then the second, using the most delicate pressure. An additional controlled squeeze and a baby rosebud materialized. Wiping his brow, the chef looked with longing at the large wedding cake awaiting his attention. Smaller is not necessarily easier.

The small diamond on my friend's hand displayed the concerted efforts of many skilled craftsmen. A natural diamond is not in and of itself such a beautiful thing. To the untrained eye it might appear as little more than a hunk of glass crystals, but in the hands of a master, that rock is transformed. Facets are discovered by careful examination. Only after extraneous portions of the stone are split off is the rare beauty within the stone exposed. After the diamond is cut, skilled jewelers match the shape, style, and brilliance of the cut diamond to an appropriate setting. Light must pass under, around, and through its many facets to reflect and magnify the stone's brilliance.

The diamond didn't fall from the sky flawlessly cut and adeptly set. Neither did the couple begin their engagement without some preparation for the undertaking. Each one's willingness to set aside personal gratification for the other's needs was a deliberate choice made upon their commitment to each other. Both partners held Christ at the center of their relationship and looked to him for direction. This was the setting that allowed their many facets to shine with unrestrained brilliance.

> Do not be conformed to this world, but be transformed by the renewing of your minds, so that you may discern what is the will of God—what is good and acceptable and perfect.
>
> Romans 12:2

Fun Facts

Concerned about heart disease? Maybe chocolate is the answer. Phenolics, antioxidant chemicals in chocolate, stop LDL (bad cholesterol) from oxidizing. Some scientists think this may well protect us from the risk of heart disease.

According to the Indiana University School of Medicine, chocolate consumption does not in any way cause or aggravate acne. There are a few individuals who may be sensitive to items often added to chocolate (e.g., nuts or fruit), but the chocolate itself is not the culprit.[2]

41

Teenagers

I know why God delivers our children as sweet little bundles of helpless pink joy. If our first parenting experience involved a rebellious teenager, we would most likely run to the hills, screaming for mercy.

Teenagers still have the spirit of a child—but that childlike spirit gets packaged with a large dose of hormonal energy in an adult body. Now, when adults think of hormones we immediately think of sex, but hormones do a whole lot more than help us procreate. In young men they generate a desire for physical prowess. In young women there is the sudden need to nurture—and along with that an urge to eat chocolate.

So what exactly makes teenagers so difficult to raise? The desire to be good at sports and the need to nurture certainly are not bad traits. And who could argue with a person's love for chocolate? The problem is that teenagers have little aptitude for restraint. A sixteen-year-old boy may want to live, eat, and breathe ice hockey. He may plead for the best equipment and force himself beyond his immediate capacity to perform. A fifteen-year-old girl may bond with her girl-friends throughout the school day but then glue herself to the mirror or to her phone for endless hours at home. She may ignore schoolwork, family, and other matters important to her ultimate well-being. Hormones do not allow teenagers proper balance. They rob them of the ability to prioritize.

This is where adults come in. We've been there and have already paved the road out of teendom. If we want our teenagers to bear the image of adulthood, we must first be examples of godly living and then, by setting limits, help them be examples to their peers.

There is no need to fear teens' energy or even their desire to pull away from us. The challenge of every parent is to channel that motion and energy into a direction that is God-pleasing and productive. When you catch your teens doing something well or performing a good deed, praise and reward them for the action. Let them know you appreciate the unique individuals God is bringing out from within them.

> Let no one despise your youth, but set the believers an example in speech and conduct, in love, in faith, in purity.
>
> 1 Timothy 4:12

Fun Facts

The Famous and Infamous

- Napoleon reportedly carried chocolate on all his military campaigns.
- In 1785 Thomas Jefferson wrote a letter to John Adams unequivocally stating that chocolate was superior to both tea and coffee when it came to health and nutritional benefits.

- Madame de Pompadour, mistress of Louis XV, who reigned as the most powerful woman in France for nearly twenty years, is said to have owned the most expensive porcelain chocolate serving piece ever made.

- Casanova, one of the greatest romantics of all time, considered chocolate to be above even champagne in its seductive and aphrodisiac properties.

42

Pudding Paint

"Mommy, can we go outside?" my son asked.

"You know I can't let you go out in this weather," I replied as a clap of thunder punctuated my statement.

"But we're bored!" My usually energetic son's shoulders sagged like a pair of old panty hose.

"How about I make some pudding?"

His younger brother came running from the other room, barely able to control his excitement. "Pudding? Can we paint?"

"Sure, why not." I returned his smile.

The boys hurried to clear the table while I readied the kitchen supplies.

I couldn't help but remember how pudding painting began in our home. My oldest son had been recovering from a tonsillectomy and, being the good mother that I am, I made warm pudding to soothe his aching throat. To add a measure of cheer, I placed a few nonpareils in the shape of a smiley face on the smooth surface of the chocolate pudding. I can still see his fingers all covered with chocolate as he picked up each little candy and popped it into his mouth. Then, as my reward, he dipped his fingers into the pudding and traced a smiley face onto the tray. I could have handed over a reprimand for this gesture, whisking out a paper napkin to wipe the tray clean. Instead, the two of us spent the afternoon laughing, licking our fingers, and drawing everything from kittens to motorbikes.

Today I would take pleasure in my sons' fanciful imaginations as my youngest called out, "Mommy, come see what I made!" and I would enjoy the hum of my older boys as their chocolate fingers inspired dragons and warriors. What I did not foresee was the strange question from my perceptive middle child.

I added a drop of red food coloring to the dish of vanilla pudding and stirred the mixture until it turned a lovely carnation pink. Then I carried it over to our waxed-paper-lined kitchen table.

"Why do you let us make a mess?" Alan asked. "Keith's mom would never let us paint with pudding."

When my son posed this question, I first wondered if he was talking to himself. His eyes never left the masterpiece before him, and his words fell so softly that they could have been mistaken for a prayer.

I reached for a bowl of green pistachio pudding and quietly sat down next to him. When I began my own artistic endeavor, Alan raised his beautiful blue eyes to mine. A reply was apparently expected. How could I explain to a five-year-old that his usually sane mother would, in this case, allow her kitchen to become the stage for antics unacceptable under other circumstances?

I took a deep breath and simply told the truth. "Alan, there are more important things in this world than always having a clean kitchen."

His slow, sweet smile beamed his approval. "Mommy, I made you flowers, see?"

His pudgy little fingers pushed the waxed paper toward me. An assortment of pudding colors swirled into the prettiest bouquet a mother could lay eyes on. I dipped my index finger into the chocolate pudding and swiped a bit onto the tip of his nose. Giggling, he unsuccessfully attempted to lick the bit off with his tongue. Not to be outdone, my oldest laughed, then marked his own face with chocolate, imitating a football lineman ready for the big game.

Our conversations that rainy afternoon ran a gamut of topics. I used my finger paint to illustrate stories of great men like King David and the apostle Paul. My kids responded with portraits of playground giants and ministering Sunday school teachers.

I don't know if my adult children remember the pudding finger painting sessions, but I have little doubt that the truths planted in their hearts have taken root. The time I spent cleaning that messy kitchen was well rewarded.

> I have no greater joy than this, to hear that my children are walking in the truth.
>
> 3 John 4

Pleasant Pastime

Pudding Paint

Mix one batch of instant chocolate pudding, two batches of instant vanilla pudding, and one batch of instant pistachio pudding and divide each into small bowls. Add a drop of food coloring (your choice) to one of the vanilla puddings. Cover snack trays or a table with waxed paper. Have children wear old clothing or an adult's old shirt over their play clothes. Allow children to finger paint to their hearts' content.

Note: It's a good idea to make an extra batch of pudding to be eaten later.

43

Feel Good

That day demanded every ounce of my energy. On top of a rough week, I was finishing off a challenging month. The sheerest of threads held my sanity intact. I had no idea why God placed so many trials in my life, but I was eager to have it over. The way things were going, household projects were doomed to failure the second I put my finger to them. Writing assignments sat in a stagnant pool with a multitude of half-finished manuscripts and incomplete thoughts. My personal relationships were deteriorating with lightning speed. If I so much as grasped a thought, the inspiration was sure to crumble under my touch.

What I needed was for someone to hold me tight and whisper, "Louise, you are important. It doesn't matter what projects you complete or what lame thoughts you hold. I love you anyway." But no one came forward. What did I do? I did what millions of women before me have done—I turned to comfort food.

I was eating alone that night. My husband was working late, and my boys were busy with various activities. I was too occupied that week to grocery shop, and my cupboards echoed a hollow lament as they closed. I was left with few choices. I could make a sandwich with a lonely slice of processed cheese food or stop for convenience food. I opted for the latter.

The vinyl-covered booth seats at the pizzeria were cold and discomforting. As I finished the single slice of pepperoni pizza, my physical appetite was sated, but my soul was unsatisfied. That was when the chocolate craving came. It started as a flicker of reflection, a mere impression—but as I waited for the waitress to bring the check, my mind lingered on the notion of a chocolate dessert. Soon that wisp of a thought turned into greater longing, and within minutes it became desperation. My need for chocolate raged like a fire that threatened to consume me.

I ran through a short list of chocolate possibilities and concluded that a sundae with hot fudge and peanut butter sauce would most readily fill my yearning.

As the girl set my dish in front of me, I could see the dark fudge sliding down the mountain of ice cream. Golden peanut butter swirled around it like the crown on a chocolate queen. I dug in and savored the first bite. Its rich, sweet taste truly lifted my downtrodden spirit. But before long I found the dish empty.

I stared into the bottom of the bowl and scraped at the last teaspoon of sauce. The spoon froze halfway to my lips. *Once I consume this, my pleasure will be over. What then?* I thought. There wasn't enough fudge in the universe to alter my self-pity at that moment.

I put the spoon back down. If eating the last spoonful wasn't going to help, then why bother? I needed a bigger, better, and more permanent fix. After paying the bill, I hurried to my car.

The problem was that my spirit, not my body, was looking for nourishment. I sat behind the steering wheel, unable to place the key in the ignition.

Father? Are you there? Help me.

A stream of comforting tears came slow and steady. As each fell, the weight of my problems seemed to fall away with them. God still sat on his throne, and he cared about me. It did not matter if the world tossed me aside—I was once again in my Father's arms.

> Therefore let us draw near with confidence to the throne of grace, so that we may receive mercy and find grace to help in time of need.
>
> Hebrews 4:16 NASB

Recipe to Relish

Haystacks

1 cup chocolate chips
1 tsp. shortening
1 cup flaked coconut

Place chips and shortening in a microwave-safe bowl and heat on high for 1 minute, stirring after 30 seconds. If necessary, microwave for an additional 30 seconds or until smooth. Add coconut. Using a tablespoon, mound the mixture in stacks on a waxed-paper-lined cookie sheet. Refrigerate until firm. Makes approximately 1 dozen haystacks.

For extra fun, scatter with multicolored sprinkles while the chocolate is still warm.

44

Cabbage Truffles

The dessert buffet held many delectable treats, but there was one item that drew special attention. Large cabbage leaves encircled the heart of the piece, while shortbread cookies lay scattered about like lily pads around a swan. Individuals flocked to the table in an attempt to taste the unique offering. Cabbage and cookies are not often served together, much less as a dessert, but in this particular case, they were well suited for each other. You see, the cabbage leaves were made of dark chocolate, and the center held a rich chocolate truffle.

I wondered aloud how my sister had created the leaves. The edges curled ever so gently outward, and the relaxed form of each ridge and ruffle proved most realistic.

"The reason the leaves look so natural is because I use real cabbage leaves to mold the chocolate," she said, laughing.

"You're kidding," I said, my jaw dropping slightly. "How do you do that?"

"It's easy. You can use almost any nontoxic leaf—cabbage, mint, fruit tree, even oak. You wash and dry them thoroughly, then coat the back of each leaf with a layer of melted chocolate. Cool it, coat it again, cool it, and repeat. When the chocolate is thick enough, you very carefully remove the leaf, and, voila, you have a replica in chocolate. To create the appearance of a whole cabbage, I make a large truffle and place chocolate replicas of the outer leaves around it. Guests dip their cookies into the sweet, truffle center, and they can break off bits of the leaves as well."

"Amazing."

"Not really. Chocolate is great for taking the shape of anything it comes in contact with. It simply needs time to cool and multiple applications to make it strong enough to retain the shape on its own."

Most people need more than one application of a lesson before we're finished too, I thought.

Just as a good teacher provides numerous addition, subtraction, and multiplication problems before moving her students on to division, God gradually increases the difficulty of my tasks. Multiple applications may be needed before I take on the image of Christ, but I am looking forward to the sweet results.

> Put these things into practice, devote yourself to them, so that all may see your progress.
>
> 1 Timothy 4:15

Fun Facts

Chocolate in any language tastes as sweet:

English—chocolate
Armenian—schokolat
French—chocolat

German—schokolade
Italian—cioccolata
Norwegian—sjokolade
Portuguese—chocolate
Russian—shokoladno
Spanish—chocolate

45

How Much

While finishing dessert at a local diner, a friend shared some interesting information.

"Did you know that in 1988 Americans ate more than three billion pounds of chocolate? That comes to about twelve pounds per person per year," she announced.

"Where did you hear that?" I asked, my eyebrows rising at the thought.

"I heard it on the news. They said that the statistics came from the U.S. Department of Commerce and the Chocolate Manufacturers Association. Do you think it's true? Do you think we eat twelve pounds of chocolate a year?"

"I don't doubt it. And keep in mind that if Americans ate twelve pounds of chocolate a year back then, it's likely that amount has increased quite a bit since."

I watched as my young friend's brow wrinkled with concern. "Why are you so worried about this?" I asked.

"It bothers me that Americans act like gluttons while the rest of the world starves. Working families in third world countries earn as little as a few dollars a month and may eat one or maybe two inadequate meals per day." My young friend's crestfallen face reflected her deep concern as she continued. "I've had such a case of the 'guilts.' I mean, just look at me—even though I left food on my dinner plate, I ordered this ice cream for dessert. What kind of person orders dessert while other people go hungry?"

Her head hung low, and I reached across the table for her hand. "Look at me."

Her gaze moved to my face, but her eyes refused to meet mine.

"It isn't your fault that you were born into a wealthy country. Jesus said the poor would always be with us until his return. You are responsible for honorably using the gifts God gives you. Do you think you do that?"

"I try," she said, a small ray of hope entering her eyes.

"Good. Now do more than try—pray. Ask God to show you where you should use the money and talent he gave you. God is a lot bigger than you seem to think. He fed five thousand people with five loaves and two fish. He can and will provide for those who call on him. Now, his answer may not be to give them all hot fudge sundaes, but God does promise to provide everything people need, and he promises to walk right alongside them when trouble comes into their lives."

"But I don't want someone else to starve while I eat ice cream!" my friend said, stifling a sob.

"I know, but we have to trust that God knows what he's doing. What if some rich philanthropist decided he couldn't stand being rich while others were poor? Even though he ran his businesses respectably, set up college scholarships, tithed to his church, and supported numerous soup kitchens and prison ministries, he felt he wasn't doing enough. So he gave all his money away and lived in a hovel. Whom could he help there? God does have a plan. Sometimes that means we get gifts like ice cream sundaes. Sometimes it means we lose everything the world offers only to discover that we are still rich in Christ. It isn't about our 'stuff.' With or without wealth, we need to follow Christ. Do you understand?"

"I think so," she answered, a smile finally creasing the corner of her mouth. "I guess it's wrong to complain about bad circumstances that come our way, because God allows them for a reason . . . and it's just as wrong to snub the good things God brings into our lives, because they are gifts from his hand too."

"That's it. Whether we are rich or poor is really irrelevant. Everything, and I mean everything, happens with the full knowledge of our almighty God."

> Will you condemn one who is righteous and mighty, . . . who shows no partiality to nobles, nor regards the rich more than the poor, for they are all the work of his hands?
>
> Job 34:17, 19

Fun Facts

Most of us don't need a reason to eat chocolate, but if you do, I offer you the following days of chocolate celebration:

American Chocolate Week—March 14–20
National Chocolate Day—October 28
National Chocolate Day—December 28
National Chocolate Day—December 29
National Milk Chocolate Day—July 28
National Bittersweet Chocolate with Almonds Day—November 7
National Chocolate Mint Day—February 19

National Chocolate Chip Day—May 15
National Chocolate Éclair Day—June 22
National Chocolate-Covered Anything Day—
   December 16
National Chocolate-Covered Raisins Day—March 24
National Chocolate Custard Month—May 1–31
National Chocolate Pudding Day—June 26
National Chocolate Ice Cream Day—June 7
National Chocolate Milkshake Day—September 12[3]

46

Mouth Feel

The moment the bittersweet morsel crossed my lips, something exquisite ensued. I felt the once-hard chunk of chocolate give itself over to me. As a silky softness spread to the back of my throat, that one sweet note of flavor invaded my senses and rivaled the chords of angelic choirs.

Fine chocolate is the only food that melts at exactly the temperature of the human mouth. Because of this, the instant it is placed on the tongue, your brain receives a glorious message. Chocolatiers call this characteristic "mouth feel," and because of the satisfaction it brings, they consider it one of the more important aspects of a quality chocolate.

I can't say that everything I've consumed over the years has given me such pleasure. One hot afternoon last summer comes to mind. When Friday arrived I rushed out of the office, eager to get home and put my feet up for a few minutes before beginning my weekend chores. When I opened the car door, the trapped hot air hit me like a campfire fueled with gasoline. I slid into the driver's seat but left the door ajar and rolled down the windows, hoping to moderate the temperature. A tiny ache that had begun behind my eyes now spread to my temples and tore at the back of my neck. My head throbbed, I was exhausted, and the car's air-conditioning seemed not to care one bit that I was on the verge of combustion. I closed the car door, cranked the air up to "max," and began scouring my purse for some aspirin.

"Aha!" I fairly shouted when two lint-infested but still serviceable aspirin made their appearance.

Only one problem remained—how to swallow those pills. The water bottle I'd forgotten to bring into the office that morning mocked me with its tepid contents. I squirmed uncomfortably. I could go back into the office and get a beverage from the machine, but those few minutes seemed too long to wait for the relief I hoped the aspirin would afford. I set my jaw and decided to be brave. I tossed the pills into my mouth and swallowed hard, hoping my saliva would be sufficient to get them down. It was not. The pills stuck in my throat. I gagged. Grabbing for the previously spurned water, I attempted to dislodge the trapped pills. I felt the nasty water work the bitter aspirin past my windpipe and down my gullet. The acidic pills burned my throat, and a multitude of war drums beat steadily in my head the rest of the ride home.

Bitter pills, bitter people, bitter words—all burn their way into our memories. What is the remedy to things so inhospitable? The sweet taste that is ours when we spend time with God. If you are trying to swallow some of life's bitter pills, try spending time in the presence of the King of Kings. His love is as smooth and sweet as melting chocolate.

> David was in great danger; for the people spoke of stoning him, because all the people were bitter in spirit for their sons and daughters. But David strengthened himself in the LORD his God.
>
> 1 Samuel 30:6

Pleasant Pastime

Chocolate Spoons

heavy plastic spoons (ones with thick, smooth edges work best)
milk chocolate
white chocolate
chocolate sprinkles and colored sugar
waxed paper
cellophane wrap
ribbon

Melt the white chocolate and the milk chocolate in separate bowls using your microwave.

Dip the bowl-shaped portion of half of your plastic spoons in the white chocolate. Then dip the bowl-shaped portion of the remaining spoons in the milk chocolate.

After dipping, place spoons on waxed paper, bowl side up, and let them set completely.

When the chocolate is cool, dip the white chocolate spoons in milk chocolate and dip the milk chocolate spoons in white chocolate. To create an interesting effect, dip each spoon only halfway up the bowl of the spoon the second time.

Place each spoon on clean waxed paper.

After the chocolate sets for 5 minutes (still soft) gently dip each spoon in chocolate sprinkles or colored sugar.

When the chocolate is dry to the touch, wrap individual spoons in cellophane wrap and tie each with a pretty ribbon.

47

Refreshment

I locked my fingers and stretched my arms high above my head. Neck cracking, joints creaking, I stood and flexed my knees slightly. My wheeled office chair slid backward and thumped against the desk, its sound echoing through the empty building. It was still early, but I'd already put in an hour at the office. I walked slowly toward the third floor window and watched a small bird in a nearby tree hop from branch to branch. He seemed so full of energy even though he was going nowhere in particular. I wondered if a brief walk around the building might not do me some good. I stretched again, willing blood to my extremities, before glancing at my watch.

No time for a walk, I thought, *but a strong cup of coffee would sure take the edge off this fatigue.*

I headed toward the break area and rummaged through the cabinets. The sound of cupboard doors clapping against empty shelves was my only reward. I returned to my desk and plopped back into my chair no better off than when I began.

The numbers on my computer screen danced as my tired eyes struggled to focus. Without some assistance it would be difficult, if not impossible, to get through the morning.

The time had come for action. I poked through my desk drawers and finally came upon a packet of gourmet hot chocolate.

Well, I thought, *it's not coffee, but it is hot and sweet and it does contain a measure of caffeine. Maybe this will do the trick.*

The sweet scent that drifted to my nostrils as I stirred the contents of the mug into hot water sent my toes to tapping. Its frothy topping and rich color stimulated my senses. My lips approached the cup cautiously, testing the hot liquid by first taking small sips of the warm foam. When I grew accustomed to the temperature, I drank deeply, emptying the mug in short order. I closed my eyes, waiting for . . . I don't know what. A miraculous surge of energy? A flash of youth? Satisfaction was not to be mine.

Most people would agree that humans need periodic sources of refreshment. When we are hungry, we eat. When we are tired, we sleep. When we are restless, we seek entertainment. But do we give our bodies what they truly crave, or are we willing to settle for cheap substitutes?

When our spirits need refreshment, do we confuse spiritual hunger, fatigue, and restlessness with other things? I know people who fly from party to party, hoping that just around the next corner they'll find a soul mate to complete their lives. Others look for renewal by acquiring hobbies, doting on grandchildren, or putting in more effort at the office—but none of these things fully satisfy. When we are spiritually hungry, only spiritual food will refresh us.

There is nothing wrong with hot chocolate, just as there is nothing wrong with spending time with family, learning new things, or putting our best foot forward at work. It is only when these things are moved to positions of importance they were never meant to hold that we are left unsatisfied. Spiritual drought requires that we fill our spirits with the presence of God—nothing more and nothing less will work.

For I satisfy the weary ones and refresh everyone who languishes.

Jeremiah 31:25 NASB

Recipe to Relish

Whipped Cream Substitute

As an alternative to a whipped cream garnish, try whipping 1 can of chilled evaporated skim milk with 1 tablespoon of unsweetened cocoa powder for an interesting chocolate topping.

48

Taking Shape

The rich brown liquid ran like a silken thread from my friend's pastry bag. As it fell into the little chocolate molds, a few droplets of sweetness made their way onto the plastic between the cavities. These formed strange, irregular motifs amid the soldierlike repetition of the chocolate-filled molds.

"How long before the chocolates are set?" I asked.

"Oh, we'll refrigerate them for a bit, and they should be ready in less than an hour."

I silently inserted more paper sticks into the next set of molds. Soon they would be transformed into fun-ready chocolate pops. Other volunteers readied cellophane bags and cut the curling ribbon, adding flourish to our presentation.

"Do you think the kids will appreciate all the work we put into these?" I asked the parent in charge. Small beads of sweat ran along her already damp hairline, giving ample evidence of a morning spent in a hot kitchen. Her eyes crinkled as a smile rose to her face.

"Probably not—but I'll know." She turned toward one of the other volunteers and asked, "Would you get another batch out of the fridge?"

I watched as the woman gently popped out an array of chocolate music notes. Bits of excess chocolate that solidified outside the molds joined the pile, as well as one broken note. I gathered the usable pops onto a tray and asked, "What should I do with this extra chocolate?"

"Put it back in the melting pot. We'll use it again," she said without a second glance.

The volunteer manning the pot looked over her shoulder and said, "Wouldn't it be nice if we could just make over all those parts of our lives that came out wrong?"

I laughed right along with the rest, but as I watched her stir the fluid brown sweetness I saw in it deeper reflections of God's plan. Remolding broken chocolate is not unlike what God can do with our lives. He takes broken sinners and remakes them. We become new creatures when we put ourselves into his capable hands.

> And the vessel he was making of clay was spoiled . . . and he reworked it into another vessel, as it seemed good to him.
>
> Jeremiah 18:4

Pleasant Pastime

Chocolate Clay

American pastry chefs invented this recipe and have been using delicious edible clay to make garnishes and unique decorations for many years.

10 oz. chocolate (chopped or chips)
⅓ cup light corn syrup

Melt the chocolate in a microwave-safe bowl for 1 minute. Stir. If the chocolate is not completely melted, return to the microwave for 30 seconds at a time and stir. Add the corn syrup and stir once again. Pour the mixture onto a large sheet of waxed paper on a jelly roll pan or cookie sheet. Spread the chocolate with a spatula (or your fingers), creating an even ½-inch layer. Cover loosely with a second sheet of waxed paper and let it sit for at least two hours or overnight. The clay will stiffen slightly.

When you are ready to use the clay, slice a portion off and knead it as you would any clay. It will become pliable as you work with it. This is best used in a cool environment.

Making a chocolate rose

Make 10 marble-size balls out of chocolate clay. Place the balls on clean waxed paper about 1 inch apart. Press your thumb into each ball to create a flat disk about the size of a quarter. Remove 1 disk and curl it into a conelike shape, narrow at the top and wider at the bottom. Wrap the next disk around the opening of the cone, and the third disk at the back of the cone. You've just created a rose bud.

Continue adding disks, which will look like petals. Continue to layer them to create a rose in bloom. Use these roses to decorate a cake or to make chocolate party favors. They will harden after a few days and can be saved by storing them in a cool, dry place.

49

Clutching Tight

I pulled my legs under me like a cat settling on a hearth. With my ever-present cup of coffee snuggled between warm hands, I sipped quietly while my family discussed a sundry of topics. My oldest son and his wife were visiting from Virginia, and while we conversed, time paused in its relentless trek forward. Years long past returned in all their glory as we reminisced, and, somehow, recalling the past helped me put the present in perspective.

"We brought you a little gift from our last vacation, Mom," my son JC said as he held out a small box. I took it from him with anticipation.

"You didn't have to do that . . . but I'm glad you did," I joked. I opened the box and discovered a bright blue coffee mug covered in dancing candy-coated figures.

"Oh, how cute! And look—chocolate too!" I pulled out a package of the sweets that were tucked inside.

"Believe it or not, Mom, we found an entire store that sold nothing but M&Ms. You could get the candy in colors they don't sell anywhere else."

My daughter-in-law, Roni, added, "With your love for both chocolate and coffee, we figured this was the perfect gift."

"You got that right," I replied and turned to JC, who now wore the broadest of grins. "So out with it. Why the silly grin?"

"I was just remembering that trip Alan and I took to Maine with Oma and Opa."

"Just the two of you?"

"Yup . . . I think that was right after Tim was born, and they took us back to Maine for a few weeks of vacation to give you a break. Do you remember that, Alan?"

JC ducked as Alan tossed a pillow at his head.

"Hmm, so what happened?" I asked, coaxing the story out.

"Well, Oma brought a bag of M&Ms with her. I guess she figured she could keep us quiet in the car if she kept us happy. Alan and I were discussing something in the back seat."

"You mean you were fighting about something," my husband interjected.

"No, just discussing rather loudly," JC joked in return. "Anyway, Oma told us to stop it and gave us each a handful of M&Ms."

JC turned to Alan, whose large, muscular frame now stood only inches from his brother. Eyes sharp, muscles tense, he seemed ready to pounce.

"OK, so what happened?" I asked innocently.

Alan jumped in, "Let's just say that the phrase 'They melt in your mouth, not in your hand' didn't apply."

JC let out a hearty laugh. "That's an understatement. I guess Alan thought he'd be smart and save the candy for later. He closed his little fist around it and held on tight. I didn't even notice right away. Oma and Opa made a rest stop not long after Oma handed out the candy. As we were getting out of the car, Alan opened his hand, and there sat a fistful of mushed chocolate. Oma started right in wiping his hands, and, of course, Alan began crying because now he couldn't have his chocolate. At that point Opa asked Alan why he would do such a thing. Alan was trying to pull away from

Oma so he could keep his chocolate, and Oma was hanging on to his shirt, trying to clean him up. It was like watching a three-ring circus!"

I already suspected the answer, but I felt required to ask, "And you? What were you doing?"

My eldest son's blond head fairly shook with glee as he replied, "I, of course, was laughing my head off."

"Hey," Alan offered in his defense, "I was only four years old. What do you expect?"

I've seen adults act like a four-year-old child when it comes to their relationship with God. They clutch the remnants of the Father's gifts in their fists and insist on keeping the mess even after rendering it useless. How much better when we leave our hands open so we can enjoy the sweetness of his gifts.

> Every generous act of giving, with every perfect gift, is from above, coming down from the Father of lights.
>
> James 1:17

Recipe to Relish

Mocha Blast Shake

1½ cups cold coffee
2 cups milk
¼ cup chocolate syrup
¼ cup sugar

Brew 1½ cups of double-strength coffee. Allow it to cool and then pour it into ice cube trays. Freeze overnight. Place cubes, milk, sugar, and syrup in a blender. Process until smooth. Pour into tall glasses. Serves 4.

50

A Name's a Name

According to Merriam-Webster, a misnomer is the "use of a wrong name" or a "wrong name or designation."[4] Sitting here enjoying one of my favorite desserts, I can't think of anything to which this more aptly applies than Boston cream pie. Someone unfamiliar with the actual product might conjure up a vision quite different from its reality.

For the few who are unfamiliar with it, Boston cream pie is a simple yet delectable culinary marvel that consists of a generous deposit of sweet pastry cream wedged between two layers of light sponge cake. The top is then glazed with a lavish coat of bittersweet chocolate. If it were up to me to name this cake, I might just call it "heaven's cake."

Curiosity about its name led me to a bit of research on its origins. It seems that back in the early days of Boston, a chef of some renown took it upon himself to modify a cake only described as a "Boston favorite." The original, a horizontally sliced single-layer cake filled with pastry cream and dusted with powdered sugar, found itself topped instead with melted chocolate. As word of this tasty treat spread, patrons swarmed the restaurant for the newly dressed sweet that we today know as Boston cream pie.

So why did they call it a pie? That answer was simple. Early in the history of the colonies, a variety of baking pans was not available to every restaurateur. Cakes were often baked in the pie tins at hand—and thus they too were called pies. I doubt that the American populace will be moved to change the name of this famous dessert, but it did make me reflect on the importance of a name. Before my children were born, my husband and I agonized over the possibilities of names. We quickly agreed that if God blessed us with a daughter, she would be given the name Grace, but when it came to boys' names, our discussions ran long and heated. The meaning of a name was important to me. Its simplicity was an issue for my husband. As it turned out, God blessed us with three boys, and with each pregnancy the battle began afresh. A child's name may reflect many things. A parent's expectations, the family's heritage, and current cultural trends are often considered when parents choose a name for their child.

Imagine two infants lying side by side in a hospital nursery. The first sweet face that smiles from his swaddling blanket bears the name Frewyn. A nearly identical innocent face in the next bassinet bears the name Fred. The labels they are given will in some way shape each young man. Neither name is innately good or bad. They do, however, carry with them family hopes, dreams, and ideals.

When God's Son was sent to earth as an infant, God carefully chose his name. This child came from a heavenly palace but would be born in an earthly barn. His name needed to reflect the regal birthright of his father as well as the human life he would lead. With each utterance of his name God wanted his Son to be reminded of the task for which he was born. The name he chose was the Hebrew name Yeshua, which means "savior." We've come to know him by his Greek name, Jesus.

She will bear a son, and you are to name him Jesus, for he will save his people from their sins.

Matthew 1:21

For a child will be born to us, a son will be given to us; and the government will rest on His shoulders; and His name will be called Wonderful Counselor, Mighty God, Eternal Father, Prince of Peace.

Isaiah 9:6 NASB

Recipe to Relish

Boston Cream "Quick Cake"

1 ready-made pound cake
1 box instant white chocolate or vanilla pudding
1 cup chocolate chips
1 tsp. vegetable shortening

Mix the pudding according to the package directions and allow it to cool. Melt the chips and shortening in a microwave-safe bowl on full power for 30 seconds. Stir. Repeat until the chocolate is smooth. Set aside to cool slightly. Slice the pound cake horizontally to make three layers. Spread half the pudding between each of the layers. After placing the remaining layer on the cake, slowly spread the chocolate across the top. Chill and serve.

51

Comfort Food

Nearly everyone has one—some favorite childhood food we crave when we are lonely. A special taste we gravitate toward when we hurt. A food that brings solace when the world spins out of control and the fragile threads holding our lives together snap like twigs underfoot. Chocolate fits this bill more often than not as we revel in memories of warm chocolate chip cookies served by a kindhearted mother. Thoughts of the woman who smoothed out the rough places in life flood over us when we can't fix our own problems.

At this moment I am looking for comfort from a misery known as the common cold. Even as I write this, I down capsules filled with the most advanced medication in an effort to alleviate my suffering.

But it is the memories of my mother that eventually comfort me as I wrap myself in her hand-crocheted pink-and-white cocoon. Laptop computer balanced on one knee and my cat warming the other, I sip hot cocoa and dream, strangely enough, of Krepfel. This fried Austrian/German doughnutlike wonder is the epitome of comfort food when served with a cup of steaming hot chocolate on a cold day. The modern doughnut cannot compare to a fresh Krepfel set by loving hands on a small plate coated with coarse sugar for dipping. Through clogged sinus passages I strain to catch the scent of the sweet yeast dough my mother would set to rise in our warm oven. My ears strain to hear her call me to afternoon Kaffe Zeit, where the scent of frying oil would still mix with the perfume of the Krepfel she would serve.

Comfort comes from food only because of what we associate with it. I think some people attend church because they confuse a peaceful environment with a peaceful soul. Memories of candlelit choir concerts soothe emotions. Hymns remind us of friends and family long gone, and the faith of our parents may warm the recesses of our minds. I don't think it is bad to have these thoughts and feelings, but God wants to give us so much more when we come to his house. He wants us to have faith in the here and now, and he does not want us to settle for pleasant memories alone. He pleads to bind our wounds and asks that we rejoice with his angels. Some people seek food for comfort and church for nothing more than false reassurance and sentimentality. These are counterfeits—I want the real thing.

I think I'm going to stop dreaming about comforting food and give my mom a call.

> In the day of my trouble I call on you, for you will answer me.
>
> Psalm 86:7

Recipe to Relish

Easy Chocolate Truffles

¾ cup butter (do not use margarine or other substitute)
¾ cup unsweetened cocoa powder
1 can (14 oz.) sweetened condensed milk
1 Tbsp. vanilla extract
extra unsweetened cocoa powder

Melt the butter over low heat in a heavy saucepan. Add the ¾ cup cocoa powder and stir until the mixture is smooth. Add the sweetened condensed milk, stirring constantly. Continue to heat until the mixture thickens and has a glossy finish.

Remove from heat and stir in the vanilla. Cover with plastic wrap and refrigerate for at least four hours or until firm.

Using a melon baller or a small spoon, scoop small portions of the chilled truffle mixture into your hand. Quickly roll the mixture into 1¼-inch balls and then roll each ball in the extra cocoa powder. Refrigerate until firm (1 to 2 hours). Store in a sealed container in the refrigerator.

52

Humble Pie

Although the lavish dinner satisfied our physical hunger, my friends and I eagerly awaited that flourish that gratifies something hidden within the soul of humanity—dessert. We watched as the server wheeled to our table a multitiered dessert cart laden with a sizeable assortment of taste-tempting pleasures. We took our time choosing between pies built high with juicy fruit fillings, white chocolate mousse scattered with plump fresh raspberries, warm apple crisp smelling of sugar and cinnamon, and, of course, a classic multilayered chocolate cake topped with a delightful mocha icing. With patience beyond his young years, the server answered our many questions. He offered alternative calorie-light selections and made recommendations based on the chef's knowledge and his own palate. His concern for our pleasure was surpassed only by his interest in sharing his expertise.

At the server's urging I chose a pale mocha mousse drizzled with bittersweet chocolate. The chef, I was told, used a special technique that made his mousse particularly light yet satisfying. The moment that luscious cream crossed my lips, I knew I'd made the right choice. The sighs and comments of my friends assured me they were pleased with their decisions, but in my heart I knew that my choice, based on the waiter's recommendation, was undoubtedly the best.

The man's desire to serve the restaurant's clientele was noteworthy. He readily shared what he knew of the desserts and of their creator. He did this not to elevate himself but to help us choose what would suit us best. He took extra time with those who had dietary restrictions. When he could not answer a question, he sought the answer from others and quickly returned—no less ready to offer service despite the inconvenience.

I sipped my coffee along with a large dose of humility. I was ashamed that one so young already knew what it had taken me so long to learn. I'm sure this fellow's pay was little more than minimum wage, yet he carried out his duties with great care. I remember my father telling me often that there is no shame in the president of a company sweeping up a dirty floor—but was I such a willing servant?

Some church denominations hold regular foot-washing ceremonies. I think the symbolism of this task is beautiful, but I know that even this remarkable act can be misunderstood or misinterpreted. Those who watch the head of a denomination kneel before his congregants will most certainly hold such a man in higher esteem. But what of the pastor who month after month offers to drive a non-church-member to and from his job? Do we think him a fool for wasting his time? Or do we imagine him a good farmer—planting seeds, watering soil, awaiting the move of the Spirit as the seed takes root? What about the deacon's wife who quietly cleans the church toilets everyone else has complained about? Should she be chastised and told this is not for her to do? Or does her act motivate us to roll up our sleeves and scrub the church kitchen?

May God grant me the eyes to see the needs of those around me.

> The greatest among you will be your servant. All who exalt themselves will be humbled, and all who humble themselves will be exalted.
>
> Matthew 23:11–12

Fun Fact

Milton S. Hershey, the founder of the Hershey empire, started his business with a borrowed $150 in 1898. By 1900 he was an acclaimed millionaire. Although he and his wife were childless, Hershey had a love for children and in 1909 established the Milton Hershey School, an extraordinary school for boys who had lost one or both parents. Upon his death in 1945 the following eulogy was delivered by Rev. John H. Treder: "The life of Milton Hershey will always be an inspiration in the final triumph of records of perseverance, determination, and pure hard work over failure."

53

Upside-Down Worries

The sneeze that threatened to explode from within me tickled my throat and stung my eyes unmercifully. My hands grabbed for the box of tissues I'd flung on the passenger seat of my car, but with the next turn the box slid just out of my reach.

"Ahhrah!" The animal-like sound that escaped was filled with desperation. "God, just get me to work so I can take my cold medicine, and help me get through this day, *please.*"

Another turn and the tissue box slid toward me. I seized a handful of tissue and wiped at my nose, grateful for momentary relief.

Upon my arrival I headed straight for the cafeteria. Mocha java was the only thing on my mind. I'm not sure if it was my miserable cold or my joy at the sight of our brightly colored cappuccino machine, but tears again sprung to my eyes. I quickly brewed myself a cup, paid the cashier, and headed for my desk. To sit in the quiet of the morning with my cold medication and cup of comfort was all I desired. But some days were not meant to be easy. With each step I took, the floor beneath me seemed to tilt a bit more. My internal gyroscope was faltering. Hugging the wall, I made my way to a chair in our break area. Merry-go-round-like images circled me. I tipped my head back, closed my eyes, and began to silently pray.

Father, you are the solid rock on which I stand, and you calmed the stormy sea. Please stop my boat from rocking. You promise that all those who trust in you will find peace. I really need some peace right now, and I'm putting all my trust in you. Let me get through this day.

I would like to say that I opened my eyes and everything was perfect. It would have been nice if my equilibrium returned, my cold disappeared, extra pounds vanished, and years of gray hairs and wrinkles instantly faded away. That was not the case. What did happen, though, was possibly a greater miracle. My circumstances didn't change, but I didn't care.

It took a few minutes for my inner ear's stabilizing mechanism to right itself and a bit longer for the cold medication to take the edge off my sniffles. Nothing I consumed, however, could account for the feelings of love, peace, and security that surrounded me during that moment. Back at my desk I sipped my mocha java, content with the answer to my prayer. Let the waves of sickness and pain crash against my world, and let others try to force down the walls of God's fortress. I chose to look at the foundation stone, the everlasting rock that gave me life, the sheltering mountain that kept me from harm.

If you find that your world is spinning and life has flipped you upside down, steadfastly fix your gaze on God. He will hold you tight through the storm.

> Those of steadfast mind you keep in peace—in peace because they trust in you. Trust in the LORD forever, for in the LORD God you have an everlasting rock.
>
> Isaiah 26:3–4

Recipe to Relish

Coconut Pecan Chocolate Upside-Down Cake

Topping

> 1 cup finely chopped pecans
> 1 cup coconut

Cake

> 1 package chocolate cake mix
> 1 lb. powdered sugar
> 8 oz. softened cream cheese
> ½ cup softened butter

Spread the pecans and coconut in the bottom of a greased and floured 9 x 13 pan. Prepare the cake mix according to the manufacturer's directions. Pour the prepared batter over the topping spread in the bottom of the pan. In a separate bowl, mix the cream cheese, butter, and sugar. Drop large spoonfuls of the cream cheese mixture on top of the cake batter. Bake at 350 degrees for 45 minutes or until a toothpick inserted near the center of the cake comes out clean.

This cake may be eaten warm, served from the pan. If you prefer, allow the cake to cool, then invert the cake onto a platter. It is especially delicious with generous scoops of coconut ice cream.

54

The Kiss

I love everything about the candy kiss—the white paper tuft that flies like a victory flag above its silver armor, the familiar sweet scent that assails my nostrils when I first open the bag, even the faint crinkly sound that fills my ears as I unsheathe each tiny morsel. I love candy kisses.

I usually keep a candy dish on a small credenza opposite my office desk. What is the item of choice to fill that dish? Milk chocolate kisses and white chocolate hugs. In recent years, the manufacturer of these delightful bite-size bits began offering even more variety. Previously, you would find a piece of traditional milk chocolate inside each silver jacket. Today, both the wrapping and the product have more variety. Stripes indicate white chocolate, and gold foreshadows almonds. Most recently, a metallic green and silver checkerboard pattern promises mint-flavored dark chocolate. Of all the varieties, this has become my favorite. Tiny little bursts of mint-flavored chocolate formed into a playful shape and wrapped as a shiny bauble—you can't get better than that.

Because of my early-bird tendencies, there is a long span between that eye-opening cup of morning java and the afternoon lunch break. As a child I was led to believe that chocolate is not something one eats before noon. Nutritionists assure me that a piece of fruit or some crunchy fresh vegetables would serve me better as a midmorning snack, but my earthly soul longs for mint chocolates.

All I need is one, because each kiss contains quite a wallop. Simply unleashing the mint scent from its silver wrapper sends renewed inspiration to my stagnant brain. Placing the smooth, flat bottom of the kiss against my tongue carries waves of comfort to my tired limbs. One small candy kiss packs a great deal of zest.

God tells us that faith is like that—a little goes a long way. Our human minds tell us that only quantity counts. The man with the most physical prowess is the better man. The more beautiful the woman, the more womanly she is perceived. Individuals with the most wealth and power are obviously the best of the lot.

But in a place where city walls are made of transparent gold and foundations are laid using precious jewels, where time is meaningless and water quenches thirst for all eternity, it takes only a microscopic drop of faith to uproot trees and move mountains. Each time one tiny candy kiss satisfies my need, I remember one greater than me who supplies me with a faith that will move mountains.

> The Lord replied, "If you had faith the size of a mustard seed, you could say to this mulberry tree, 'Be uprooted and planted in the sea,' and it would obey you."
>
> Luke 17:6

Sweet Poetry

The Kiss

A
fine
chocolate
is a joy to be
cherished.

A
dark
chocolate is
love poured with
a caring hand.

A
milk
chocolate
is hope by way
of kindness.

A
white
chocolate
is help laced
with love.

All
chocolate
is a grand gift, an
extravagant gesture, a
kiss from heaven, a
symbol of Love.

Louise Bergmann DuMont

55

Grace

Sipping a cup of delicious black coffee, I offered my friend a piece of the chocolate pound cake I was nibbling.

"Why are you so happy this morning?" she asked innocently.

"Do you really want to know?" I asked.

"Sure. Why should you corner the market on happiness?"

"Well, I'm smiling because the morning started out absolutely miserable, but God transformed everything—he gave me a do-over."

"Wh-what?" she asked.

I leaned forward and eagerly began my story.

"Do you remember when we were kids? If you were playing a game and the ball ran afoul of a tree or a neighborhood dog interfered with your game, you could call out, 'Do-over.' This morning I desperately wanted a 'do-over.'

"My husband, John, usually finishes brushing his teeth around 5:30 a.m. That's when he gently tugs at my covers and I know it's my turn to rise and shine. For whatever reason, this morning he was running late, which, of course, meant that I was running late.

"On most days I'm out the door by 6:15, but it was already 6:30 when I grabbed my shoes, plopped into a living room chair, and began tying the laces. That was when the first disaster struck. It took only a moment for me to feel a strange dampness on my posterior. When I looked down onto the chair, I realized that the cat must have had a rough night. He'd gotten sick on my recliner."

"Oh, yuck!" my friend cried.

"Yuck is right. I rushed to the bedroom, kicked off my shoes, changed my clothes, cleaned up the living room, tossed my pants into the washer, and headed out the door, hoping to make up some time on the road. I no sooner put the key into the ignition of my car than I realized I was leaving with my fuzzy yellow slippers on."

"You're kidding."

"I wouldn't kid you about that. So I turned off the car and fruitlessly searched my purse for my house keys. It wasn't until nearly ten minutes later that I remembered tossing them on the kitchen counter instead of in my bag. I trudged around the house to the back door, where I located the spare key and reentered the house. Back in the bedroom, I once again changed my clothes because my pant legs are now soaked with the rain from the puddles left in the grass the evening before. This time I made certain I put shoes on, then grabbed my house keys and headed for the car again."

"So . . . when does the happy part come in?"

"I'm getting there. Hang on," I said, smiling. "Trying for the third time, I left my front door and started my car. I was really late, so I took off down my road a bit faster than usual and nearly ran over a group of high school kids who were sitting cross-legged in the road at the bus stop. If they'd been standing in the road, that would be one thing, but since they were sitting on the road, I barely saw them in time. Then, despite my lateness, I wasn't in such a hurry to put the pedal to the metal."

"I can only imagine."

"So I looked down at the dashboard to check my speed and realized I was practically running on fumes. I stopped for gas, and I didn't have enough money, so I paid by credit card. I then had to go to the bank. I'm meeting a friend for dinner tonight, and I needed some cash for the day. I got to the ATM, and guess what?"

"I can only imagine that it shot out hundreds of dollars. Is that what made you so happy?" She grinned.

"No, the ATM was out of money."

"No way!"

"Yup. Needless to say, I did not have either the time or the money to stop for my cup of coffee on the way to work."

"I'm still waiting to find out why you're so happy. If all that happened to me, I'd be miserable for the rest of the day!"

"Well, now comes the good part. I was driving down the highway that winds in and out of the mountains where we live, and lo and behold, the most beautiful sunrise I've ever seen came up over the mountain. The sky above me was still dark with clouds from the storm that hit last night. Everything looked unsettled—all except for the horizon where the sun was coming up. The sky, the mountains, the valley below the bridge where the river runs—it all glowed. It was as if I were viewing everything through transparent gold. All I could think of was, *Thank you, God, for making me late so I could see this.* You see, God loves me so much that he made sure I wouldn't miss the big event he was planning. I thought I was late, but God was just slowing me down so I would be right on time. When I finally got to work, he topped it all off with chocolate pound cake for breakfast. You can't get better than that."

Yes, everything is for your sake, so that grace, as it extends to more and more people, may increase thanksgiving, to the glory of God.

2 Corinthians 4:15

Fun Facts

Chocolate around the World

- **Switzerland** reportedly consumes more chocolate per person than any other country.
- The **United States of America** is the number one producer of chocolate candy in the world.
- **Ghana** is the world's largest producer of raw cocoa beans for commercial use.
- The cocoa bean was first used in beverage form by the Aztecs in **Mexico**.
- The world's largest single producer of chocolate is Cadbury of Birmingham, **England**.
- **Brazil** was the site of the first cocoa plantation.
- In the late 1900s **Belgium** reported more than 2,130 chocolate shops.
- In Paris, **France**, adults and children alike eat chocolate fish in anticipation of April Fool's Day.

56

$\mathcal{R}eminisce$

The dessert arrives, and with it my mood shifts from pleasant to pensive. Dessert signals the end. Sweets deaden the appetite and encourage the mind to turn to other things. I do not want my mind to turn from its current interest. I want to revel in the memories I share with my longtime friend. I want to step back and return to a simpler time.

When Eleanor and I first met, my biggest worries were finding new and exciting ground beef recipes to stretch our meager budget and getting our children to share their toys. There were no car or college payments to struggle with and no marketing strategies to negotiate. *Hot flashes, midlife crisis,* and *empty nest syndrome* were not even terms in my vocabulary. Traveling down the road of time together, we weathered many a catastrophe and shared many a joy.

My dessert waits patiently. I stare at the luscious blondie a la mode set before me while I fight for control of my thoughts. Drops of creamy white ice cream run like tears down the side of the still-warm white chocolate. God reminds me that my strong personality can melt others' favor as quickly as that personality can stimulate their appetite for my words.

I smile across the table at my friend, and she returns the favor. Eleanor's presence somehow makes me see the best and the worst in me. Eleanor exposes my soul. She knows I can stand strong in my faith, but she also knows my wimpy attempts to look good in front of others and my prideful nature. She knows my big mistakes and the small ones I've hidden from so many others. This makes me crave her company and makes me want to run and hide all at the same time. With Eleanor I am who I am. No pretense will work. With others I can put on my church face and talk the talk of faith, disregarding the knots in my stomach. I can hum a hymn and at the same time dawdle just enough to miss the first part of the prayer meeting.

As Eleanor levels her gaze across the melting ice cream, I know that my ruse will not work here. She sees the truth and knows my heart. Like the mother who wipes schmutz off her child's face and then plants a kiss on his forehead, Eleanor knows I'm a sinner and loves me anyway. Joy surges through me at this realization. Dessert is not the end—it is simply the crowning glory of one of many meals.

If humans have such wonderful relationships among themselves, how much greater can our relationship be with Almighty God? This can be the most intimate of all relationships. He knows every quirk and liability we possess, yet he loves us beyond all reason. What a blessing awaits those who open their hearts to the Creator.

> Thus the scripture was fulfilled that says, "Abraham believed God, and it was reckoned to him as righteousness," and he was called the friend of God.
>
> James 2:23

182

Fun Fact

Advertisement:

March 12, 1770
Boston
Gazette and Country Journal

To be sold by
JOHN BAKER
at his store in Back Street a few Bags of
the best cocoa; also choice Chocolate by
the Hundred or Smaller Quantity.

57

Genuinely Sweet

Most people think chocolate's beloved status is a result of its sweetness, but chocolate in and of itself is not sweet at all. The first consumers of chocolate, the Aztecs, ground cocoa beans to a powder and stirred this cocoa dust into water or wine. They then added chili peppers, cornmeal, and even an occasional hallucinogenic mushroom. This produced a rather bitter, biting, and often brutish beverage. That is a far cry from the sweet hot cocoa Grandma served us after we shoveled the icy snow off her walkway.

Chocolate treats of the twenty-first century taste sweet only because sugar has been added to whatever recipe is being produced. All you need to do is sample a bit of bakers' chocolate to realize that without a touch of sweetener, few individuals would enjoy their favorite chewy brownies.

A few weeks ago I met a friend for an evening of shopping. She is one of the sweetest people I've ever known, but on this night something was different.

"Which of these do you think Roni would like more?" I asked, holding up two cute T-shirts for my friend to admire.

"I don't know. Does it really matter? That girl is so tiny, anything would look great on her."

"I know, but which do you think she would *like* better."

"It doesn't matter! She lives in Virginia. If she doesn't like it she can toss it."

With a *click* I hung both shirts back on the rack. "What's the matter with you? I don't want to buy her something just so I can say I gave her a gift. I want to get her something she'll actually enjoy. You've been grumpy all night. You OK?"

My friend continued to examine the pair of slacks in her hand. She held them in midair, studying their silver studs as if she'd never seen anything so fascinating. I was about to repeat my question when she placed her hand on her hip and turned on me.

"You think you have everything so together. You work full-time, you run all kinds of ministries, and then you write books in your spare time. Well, not all of us have the perfect life. Some of us struggle with things day in and day out that you can't even fathom. Get off my case, OK?"

My jaw dropped. I watched her flip over the tag on the slacks, then move on to the next item in the rack. Passersby might have thought that nothing at all had just happened.

"I—but—I . . ." I stumbled over inadequate words. "Um . . . You want to go get a cup of coffee?"

"Sure, why not," she chirped a bit too brightly.

Over a cup of cappuccino and a slice of chocolate cake, I gathered my thoughts and approached the subject once again.

"Look, I don't know what's going on, but something's not right. Do you want to talk about it?"

I watched her face. Only a moment before it had sported a smile. Now, like a poorly manufactured mask, it began to crack, revealing the angry and distraught countenance underneath.

"It's simple. You have everything and I've got nothing. I'm so angry and so jealous, I could . . . I could just . . . *spit!*" She fairly shouted the last word.

We stared at each other for a long moment; then, as a visual image of her words came to mind, both of us started to laugh.

My friend continued, "Look, except for the jealous part, what I said isn't really true. You've worked hard to get where you are, and God has blessed me too. I just struggle so much, and things come so easily to you."

A crooked smile formed on my face as I gently reminded my friend of the trials that birthed my writing and the number of hours I put into my day job, my family, and my ministries. Her spirit seemed to lift. As my words settled onto her heart, she began to understand that having trials did not mean she was any less loved.

So often our friendly faces are little more than bitter chocolate dressed up with sugar. The only real solution is to allow God to remove our angry attitudes and replace them with his genuine sweet spirit.

> Create in me a clean heart, O God, and put a new and right spirit within me.
>
> Psalm 51:10

Cocoa Quote

After a good, complete, and copious breakfast, if we take in addition a cup of well-made chocolate, digestion will be perfectly accomplished in three hours, and we may dine whenever we like. Out of zeal for science, and by dint of eloquence, I have induced many ladies to try this experiment. They all declared, in the beginning, that it would kill them; but they have all thriven on it, and have not failed to glorify their teacher.

Brillat-Savarin (1755–1826)

58

Precious Frankincense

In years past, chocolate was a rare treat that only society's wealthiest patrons could afford. Today you will find a variety of chocolate products stacked near every checkout line, each easily affordable to most of the store's patrons. I made several chocolate purchases destined for my young men's Christmas stockings this year, but I included a less common gift as well. Tucked among the usual candy canes, men's cologne, and new toothbrushes, I placed carefully wrapped boxes of gold (in the form of chocolate coins), frankincense, and myrrh, reminders of the gifts the wise men presented to Jesus. The chocolate coins were low-cost treats, but I was surprised that the genuine myrrh and frankincense were also relatively inexpensive.

A little Internet research told me that today frankincense is sold on nearly every Middle Eastern street corner for a mere two dollars per bag, but two thousand years ago it was quite the precious commodity. The Frankincense Trail, the caravan route from harvest to market, was a carefully guarded secret that is only now, in the twenty-first century, being revealed to the general public. Bandits who successfully fell upon a frankincense caravan would have been wealthy beyond imagination. Frankincense was sold for its medicinal and restorative properties. Wealthy men and women eager to retain their youth wanted it for lotions and cosmetics, while medical personnel used it to heal everything from simple skin rashes to severe wounds.

I believe the Magi brought the Christ child many gifts that were not mentioned in Scripture. The three that were revealed were significant in that each represented a particular aspect of our Savior. The gold symbolized his status as king, frankincense was commonly used for embalming and foreshadowed his sacrificial death, and both myrrh and frankincense were used for healing and represented the healing nature of Christ.

I find it interesting that something as precious as frankincense can be treated with such disregard today. Its properties remain the same. Frankincense is still used as an astringent or antiseptic. When used in an ointment, it retains its ability to remove fine lines on a woman's aging face, and it continues to retard bacterial growth. So what brought down the monetary value of this commodity? There seems to be a simple answer. Growers and manufacturers of the product created cheaper, more advanced, easily attainable, artificial alternatives. Today frankincense is nothing more than a common Middle Eastern spice. Like chocolate, more alternatives made it less valuable.

I wonder if humans aren't treating life a little like frankincense and chocolate. Advances in medicine and technology allow us to live longer, healthier lives. Sports figures run faster and throw farther. Schools of higher education produce intellectual giants, and entrepreneurs invent gadgets that help technology race forward at a record pace. Those unable to be the best may be perceived as less than human. Those unwilling to keep up might be asked, or forced, to step out of the picture altogether.

This is not God's plan. God sees each of us as precious and valuable. The next time your worth is questioned, think about frankincense. God chose this simple spice to represent a complex aspect of his personality. If frankincense remains precious to God, so do you.

> Are not two sparrows sold for a penny? Yet not one of them will fall to the ground apart from your Father. And even the hairs of your head are all counted. So do not be afraid; you are of more value than many sparrows.
>
> Matthew 10:29–31

Fun Fact

Chocolate manufacturers use 40 percent of the world's almonds, 20 percent of the world's peanuts, and 8 percent of the world's sugar. Members of the Chocolate Manufacturers Association use about 3.5 million pounds of whole milk each day to make milk chocolate.[5]

59

Traditions

Visits with my oldest son, JC, and my daughter-in-law, Roni, are always special, but on their last trip to New Jersey I was particularly delighted. My men were going to spend the day bonding at one of those monster lumber and hardware stores. With no desire to frolic amid pipes and electrical wire, Roni and I had the entire afternoon to ourselves. Over bowls of popcorn and mugs of coffee and hot chocolate, we talked about the home she and JC would soon purchase and the room it would afford their children. This led to a revealing discussion about family traditions.

"Did I ever tell you about our Easter tradition?" I asked.

"No, tell me," Roni said as she tucked her petite feet comfortably under her and settled the popcorn bowl into her lap.

"Well, we filled the boys' Easter baskets with the usual chocolate, Easter eggs, and trinkets, but they had to go on a treasure hunt to find them. On Easter morning, a sticky note would be attached to each boy's door. On that note would be a Scripture verse that held a clue to another note. After about a dozen notes, the boys would find their baskets."

"I imagine you enjoyed writing the notes as much as they enjoyed tracking down the clues."

A frown began to crease my jaw. Coming up with unusual clues wasn't always easy or fun. Then I remembered Easter morning. I could see my three young boys dressed in crisp shirts and pressed khaki pants. Their faces beamed as their eyes eagerly searched for the next note hidden among the leaves of a potted plant or taped to the bottom of the kitchen table. A smile replaced my frown, and I continued.

"The notes got harder to write as the kids got older. They remembered some clues and answers from one year to the next. Once, JC saw the word *time* and didn't bother reading the rest of the note. He ran right to the old schoolhouse clock where a similar note had been hidden the year before. That was when I realized I needed to be more inventive."

Roni laughed. "It figures that JC would remember a short-cut when chocolate was involved!"

"You got that right, but it was worth every sleepless minute it took to come up with those clues. The kids have great memories of those days." I set down my cup and leaned forward. "So, Roni, what family traditions do you remember?"

Her eyes sparkled.

"I know this may not seem like a big deal, but every Christmas my dad would put a bag of chocolate-covered coins in our Christmas stockings. Some years our stockings might have an extra-special gift, but before we opened that, my brother and I would fish to the toe for the coins." Roni laughed again. "My brother didn't even like the chocolate."

A question tugged at the corner of my mind. "I know the chocolate in some of those coins isn't the best, so what made the coins special?"

Roni paused. Her eyes looked beyond me as if to see something in the past. "I think it was the reliability of those coins. There were a few years when Christmas didn't come with expensive gifts—but we knew those chocolate coins would be in our stockings. Other years my parents could be more generous—but even then, the coins were there. Whether times were good, bad, or in-between, Dad put those coins in our stockings. In a way, it told me that my dad would be there for me."

Her eyes once again focused on me. "JC and I have been married two years now, and last Christmas Eve Dad still had a bag of chocolate coins waiting for me."

We both smiled.

A simple gesture done with consistency speaks volumes. When a child draws a picture with chunky crayons on the back of a brown bag, Mom proudly tapes it to the refrigerator door. It tells her child he is valued beyond his ability to produce perfection.

A good-morning kiss bestowed on a spouse, no matter what his mood or health, says, "I love you—and a case of the sniffles or a grumpy attitude won't get in the way of my love."

Some things in life must change, but God steadies unstable circumstances by sending people like you and me to remind others of his unwavering love.

> For this reason I remind you to rekindle the gift of God that is within you.
>
> 2 Timothy 1:6

Fun Fact

One chocolate chip provides enough energy for a person to walk 150 feet. This means that if you eat 35 chocolate chips, you would be able to walk 5,280 feet, or one mile. If you could consume 875,000 chips, theoretically, you could walk around the world on their energy.

60

A Christmas Yet to Come

The writing assignment was simple—write a story entitled "A Christmas Yet to Come." My mind raced to visions reflective of a Charles Dickens tale. Stories that held ghostly apparitions and futuristic sagas with unexpected twists came to me in rapid succession. While I sipped my hot cocoa topped with a mound of sweet, melting marshmallows, I allowed my mind to weave the opening paragraphs of the manuscript.

My first draft was set in the year 2052. It would take place just a month short of my one-hundredth birthday as four generations of my family gathered at a Christmas reunion. The events in my story were both humorous and appropriately sappy for the season. This story was trashed shortly after I wrote a description of myself fifty years hence. No ghost of Christmas future was ever that scary.

My second attempt at a story took a different futuristic trail. On Christmas Eve in the year 2012, Christ returned. The story leads up to this event through conversations between two scholars reflecting on an ancient Aztec calendar that abruptly ended at 2012. In truth, the Aztecs felt no need to continue their calendar, since that was the year they believed the world would cease to exist. I set this "short" story aside when I found that, in my love for archaeology, I'd already written sixteen pages and had not yet neared the end of the world.

Yesterday evening I began a new story. God once again led me to fact rather than fiction, and (as he has many times in the past) he put my back up against the deadline before handing over the material.

Our youth leader clutched his clipboard like a man in need of a lifeline.

"A young man I know asked me to share a prayer request with you. Last week he found out that he will most likely not be here next Christmas."

The leader paused to let this sink into the minds of the teens.

"Where is he going?" one girl asked, taking a gulp of cola and popping a piece of chocolate chip cookie into her mouth with practiced precision.

"He may be with Jesus next Christmas. The doctors told his family he has a rare disorder and there is no cure."

The leader again paused, but this time he appeared to be gathering his thoughts.

"I would like to pray for him, and I want to ask that you pray for me as well. I'm going to see him tomorrow, and . . . I really don't know what to say to him."

A low murmur replaced the previous lighthearted chatter. We prayed for the young man and for the youth leader, but something gnawed at my insides. I kept seeing visions of old Ebenezer Scrooge with Tiny Tim perched on his shoulder. Scrooge's step was light, and snow flurries merrily danced about them. In *A Christmas Carol*, Ebenezer Scrooge saves Tiny Tim. When he purposes to keep Christmas in his heart, when he eases the burden of the poor and lame, Ebenezer is able to fix the problems of this world.

A dose of reality settled into my spirit as I thought of the many hospitals and homes sheltering terminally ill patients.

These individuals would not get well simply because someone donated a turkey and some presents.

For a brief moment I was left helpless and hopeless. Then a Scripture verse popped into my head. I don't know when I memorized it or why, but there it was—shedding hope where a moment before there was none.

> But we do not want you to be uninformed, brothers and sisters, about those who have died, so that you may not grieve as others do who have no hope.
>
> 1 Thessalonians 4:13

That in a nutshell is the story of "A Christmas Yet to Come." The first Christmas was about Christ coming to meet us. The Great Christmas Yet to Come is when we, the believers, go to meet Christ. Whether we are here on earth for his second coming to this world or we are called to meet him on the other side of death does not matter. There will be a great reunion of Christ with his people, and that will be one amazing Christmas party.

> Weeping may linger for the night, but joy comes with the morning.
>
> Psalm 30:5

Cocoa Quote

I never met a chocolate I didn't like.

Deanna Troi in *Star Trek: The Next Generation*

Notes

1. Linda K. Fuller, Ph.D., *Chocolate Fads, Folklore and Fantasies* (New York: Harrington Park Press, 1994).

2. Information on the myth that chocolate produces teenage acne was obtained from the following websites:

    http://medicine.indiana.edu/news_releases/archive_02/april_medtips 02.html

    http://www.commonconnections.com/health/QOW-chocolate&acne.html

    http://www.chemsoc.org/chembytes/ezine/1997/chockie.htm

    http://www.healthandage.com/Home/gid7=633

    http://www.betterhealth.vic.gov.au/bhcv2/bhcarticles.nsf/pages/ Chocolate?OpenDocument

3. The Bizarre Food Holidays website, http://library.thinkquest.org/2886/ food.htm#CHOCOLATE. This website was compiled by students at Hiawatha High School, Hiawatha, KS, United States, and Paxton Consolidated, Paxton, NE, United States. This information was created as a part of the 1996 Think Quest Internet Challenge.

4. Merriam-Webster Online, 2004, http://www.merriam-webster.com, s.v. "misnomer."

5. Fuller, *Chocolate Fads.*

Louise Bergmann DuMont is an author, speaker, and Young Writer's mentor. She is the acting facilitator of the North Jersey Christian Writers Group (NJCWG) and has written for numerous periodicals, journals, and newspapers. Information about Louise and her books, *Grace by the Cup: A Break from the Daily Grind* (Revell, 2003) and *Faith-Dipped Chocolate: Rich Encouragement to Sweeten Your Day* (Revell, 2004), can be found at www.louisedumont.com. Louise includes among her loves and interests a dear husband, three grown sons, a precious daughter-in-law, gifted/learning-disabled children, and science-fiction/fantasy writing. Her column *Coffee Nips* can be found at www.ringwoodbaptist.org/html/coffee_nips.html.

Nothing complements chocolate better than a hot mug of java!

A Break from the Daily Grind

grace *by the* Cup

Louise Bergmann DuMont

Take a coffee break with these caffeine-induced devotionals. Perfect to jump-start your morning or to provide an energizing boost to round out your day.